A PARISH AT WAR

HOW THE GREAT WAR AFFECTED SITLINGTON'S MEN WOMEN AND CHILDREN

Edited by
Hilary Haigh

MIDDLESTOWN WITH NETHERTON PCC
PICKARD BOOKS
2018

First published 2018

By Middlestown with Netherton PCC
in association with Rickaro Books

ISBN 978-0-95-464399-7

Address: Rickaro Books, 17 High Street, Horbury WF4 5AB
Printed by Charlesworth Press
Designed by Paul Buckley at Riasca

CONTENTS

FOREWORD

I FIRST HEARD of the establishment of the Parish At War project from my good friend, the late John Newsome, and felt then that the idea of a detailed record of the impact of World War 1 on Sitlington was a highly appropriate way of marking the centenary of this appalling conflict. The end result is a wonderful tribute to those from the Parish who made the ultimate sacrifice on behalf of their country and a very important written record of the huge significance of the war for the people of Middlestown and Netherton.

One of my most precious personal possessions is a family photograph taken at my great-grandparents' Golden Wedding party, near Wakefield, in 1901. Seated on the floor at the front are several bright-eyed young boys – relatives of mine – who all perished in the first World War. Their loss, the deaths of all those from Sitlington Parish, plus the many millions of other victims, should never be forgotten. This book is a remarkable account of the local impact of world events and a moving testimony to those who gave their lives, ensuring their continued remembrance long after the centenary commemorations.

David Hinchliffe

ACKNOWLEDGEMENTS

THIS PUBLICATION WOULD not have been possible without the encouragement of and financial assistance from the Heritage Lottery Fund, Middlestown Gala Committee and St Luke's and St Andrew's churches.

Grateful thanks are due to Carole and Richard Knowles for their professional expertise in the preparation of this book for publication and to Paul Buckley for his design.

Many people have been involved in the Parish at War project and all have played a vital part in ensuring that the heritage of the Parish of Middlestown with Netherton is remembered.

This small but enthusiastic group of researchers worked on the project with me: Christine Hewitt, John Newsome, Wendy Newsome, Brian Webb and Steve Wilson. The death of John Newsome was a severe blow to all of us.

We have been fortunate to receive contributions to the book from Adrian Barlow, Rebecca Gill, Adam Goodyear, Christine Hallett, Sue McGeever, Cyril Pearce and Steve Wilson, all of whom are experts in their own field of research.

The National Coal Mining Museum for England has been especially generous and we thank Margaret Faull, Mike Benson, Rosemary Preece, Jill Clapham and Anisha Christison for their support.

Thanks are also due to Julie Tomlinson, the staff of Middlestown Primary Academy and Iris Rodriguez, who designed the stained glass memorial panel.

Alan Wood and members of Trinity Methodist Church, Netherton; Dr Janette Martin, Bankfield Museum; Professor Paul Ward, University of Huddersfield supported the Parish at War Project.

These relations of the men who died have been generous in their support: Marlene Oakland and members of the Kaye family; David Earnshaw and members of the Earnshaw family for permission to publish Harry Moxon's letters; Audrey Parker and members of the Bowers family.

Thanks are due to Sue Earnshaw and members of Sitlington Parish Council; to Margaret Wright, Harry Hayes and members of St Luke's and St Andrew's congregations; to Shirley Jones and members of the Coxley News team; to members of the Royal British Legion and the Horbury and Ossett Phoenix Rotary Club and to the staff of West Yorkshire Archive Service and Wakefield One.

Lastly, we should like to thank our families and friends for their encouragement and support over the past months when the Parish at War Project crept into so many conversations! Any errors or omissions are, of course, our own!

Hilary Haigh and Christine Hewitt

INTRODUCTION

Hilary Haigh

OUR COMMUNITY PROJECT focused on ways to explore, conserve and share the heritage of the Great War in the Parish of Middlestown with Netherton.

In 1914 the Parish of Middlestown with Netherton comprised the townships of Middlestown, Midgley, Netherton and Overton and at the time of 1911 census, the population of the Parish was 2,876. The main employment was on the land, down the mine, in the mill, the iron foundry or the wood yard. The major landowners were Viscount Allendale, Lord Savile and George Lane Fox and Sir George Armytage.

It is not known how many men answered the call to serve their country when war was declared, but the names of 35 men are recorded on the war memorials, with the dedication '*Their Name Liveth For Evermore*'.

One hundred years later, however, little was known locally about these men and a major aim of the Project was to revive local remembrance of them and to honour their sacrifice and that of their families. This has been expressed in several ways: the restoration and conservation of the war memorial's stained glass windows; the exploration of heritage memories and contemporary sources; the exploration of life in the Parish between 1914 and 1919 and the compilation of knowledge about the men and their families.

The War Memorial, comprising three stained glass windows and a brass plaque on which were inscribed the names of men who died, was dedicated in St Luke's Church, New Road, Middlestown, on 25 September 1920. For structural reasons, however, this St Luke's Church was demolished in 1969/70 and replaced by a smaller, modern building.

The War Memorial stained glass windows from the old Church were damaged during the demolition, but the pieces were retained and stored (in inappropriate conditions) in the vestry of the present St Luke's Church. These window sections have been repaired and the War Memorial restored. The War Memorial was rededicated by Bishop Tony Robinson at a public service on 30 October 2016.

The men commemorated on the memorials were from a variety of backgrounds and places. Some of them were baptised in St Luke's Church, the Parish Church for Middlestown with Netherton, and attended the village schools, churches and chapels, several serving as Sunday School teachers, members of the choir or, in the case of Cecil Bedford and Rowland Kaye as church or chapel organists.

Evidence of their service record and their place of death and burial has been researched in the archives of the Commonwealth War Graves Commission and regimental diaries. Painstaking research in copies of the *Wakefield Express* for 1914-1918 has revealed a fund of information, including photographs of many of the men.

Workshops on war memorials, stained glass and the artist C. E. Kempe have been delivered to schoolchildren and adults, who have had the opportunity to learn about contemporary sources, such as newspapers, directories, parish records, school log books, photographs, letters and diaries in several public talks and two full day 'Lest We Forget' events at the National Coal Mining Museum for England, located in the Parish and a participant in the Project.

Middlestown Primary Academy, also a participant in the Project, held an art competition with the First World War as its theme and as part of his workshop on stained glass, Adam Goodyear created a panel from a design by one of the children. This panel, now installed in Middlestown Academy as their memorial, was dedicated at a public ceremony on 9 November 2017 by the Rev. John Geary, Priest-in-Charge of the Parish of Middlestown with Netherton.

Through personal contact and social media it has been possible to contact several relations of those named on the war memorials, one of whom, Wilfred Bowers, was commemorated by one of the 888,246 ceramic poppies in the 'Blood Swept Lands and Seas of Red' installation at the Tower of London in 2014.

Social events to disseminate information gathered have been held and articles have been published in the *Coxley News*; an exhibition has been prepared for display in the parish and this book compiled to ensure that not only will the names of those who fell 'live for evermore', but that they are remembered as real people.

As well as chapters on the men who did not return, Rachel Gill's contribution describes the Belgian families who were given refuge in the parish after they escaped from Antwerp in 1914 when their country was invaded and occupied by the German army.

Conversely, some local men, serving in the Marines, were involved in the defence of Antwerp until it was overrun and they were able to escape over the border to Holland, where they were well treated but interned in the 'British camp'. For them the war was over, and they were able to mix with the local population and enjoy leaves of absence. An account of a visit to these men by Wakefield business man Mr H. H. Gledhill appears on page 102.

A group of Austrian prisoners of war were based at Midgley and employed by Job Earnshaw in the wood yard. They constructed their own living quarters and stayed in Midgley until the end of the war.

Some references have been traced to conscientious objectors, who were housed in Wakefield prison, but employed in working parties in Horbury Bridge and the local area.

Cyril Pearce gives an introduction to the aims of conscientious objectors.

Many local men did join the colours, however. Indeed so many members of Middlestown Athletic Club joined the colours that the club's activities were suspended for the duration!

One of these men, Private Harold Davies of the Coldstream Guards, a member of the British Expeditionary Force, whose family lived on Sandy Lane, was one of the first casualties. At first he was listed as missing, but eventually was accorded the date of 29 October 1914 for his death; he was 19 years old. On that day the 1st Battalion, Coldstream Guards suffered such casualties that it had no officers left and only 80 men.

Harold's story is one of thirty-five described in the book. Each one is a story of a young life cut short in the horror of war.

Christine Hallett describes life on the battlefield and the treatment of the wounded. For those who survived the war, some wounds were lifelong. One such was Claude Brook, who taught at Netherton School. He enlisted in November 1914 and was sent to Malta, Egypt and then the Dardanelles, where he saw active service and was part of the evacuation from Gallipoli in 1915. In 1916 Mr Brook was severely wounded and had to be invalided home; he received his discharge from the army in April 1917 and resumed duties at Netherton School until his lameness obliged him to change schools temporarily.

A picture of life for the serving soldier emerges from the correspondence of Sergeant Harry Moxon, whose letters describe his training camp in Richmond and subsequent journey to France, ending with his final letter before his death. We are fortunate that these letters have been retained, telling as they do the story of one man's experience.

Family members on the Home Front supported their sons, brothers, husbands and uncles in many ways. Parcels were sent to the front containing cigarettes as well as hand knitted socks, cardigans and scarves; letters were written by family members and school children; money was raised through collections and concerts for the Red Cross, military and other charities.

Wentworth House (later Wakefield Girls' High School) was a war hospital and local people sponsored the supply of eggs, fruit and local produce. Local women, including Nurse Eliza Ann Hampshire from Netherton, worked there as VADs.

Other women worked in munitions, in shops, on the farms and in the schools. The log books for Middlestown and Netherton schools give details of women teachers being employed while male teachers were at the front and they oversaw the contributions made by the children to the war effort in the shape of letters and presents for the soldiers and collections for presents such as handkerchiefs and contributions to the war horse fund.

When at last peace came with the Armistice of 11 November 1918, in Middlestown the celebratory bonfire was lit at Town End, the place at which many of the young men who set off to fight were recruited.

For those who did not return, memorials were placed in St Andrew's Church, Netherton, St Luke's Church, Middlestown, Trinity Methodist Church, Netherton and Netherton School. The stained glass windows by the Kempe studio have been described in detail by Adrian Barlow and the process for their conservation is set out by Adam Goodyear.

As part of this project a memorial, designed by Iris Rodriguez, a student at Middlestown Primary Academy, has been installed as a memorial to all former pupils involved in any conflict.

THE PARISH
IN 1914

Hilary Haigh

IN 1914 THE Parish of Middlestown with Netherton comprised the townships of Middlestown, Midgley, Netherton and Overton.

CHURCH AND CHAPEL LIFE

The ecclesiastical parish of St Luke's, Middlestown with St Andrew's, Netherton had been created in 1878 from the mother parish of Thornhill. The parish church, dedicated to St Luke, was built on New Road, Middlestown in 1876 and the daughter church, dedicated to St Andrew, designed by the renowned London architect John D. Sedding, was opened in Netherton in 1881 with accommodation for 200 people. In 1914 the Vicar, based in Middlestown, was Rev Gavin Charles Hamilton, who was appointed to the living in 1879; his Curate, based in Netherton, was Rev. John Kaye, MA (Oxford), who had been in post since 1908.

In addition to the two Anglican places of worship, there were Primitive Methodist chapels in Middlestown (built 1886), Netherton (1890) and Overton; a United Methodist chapel in Midgley (built 1851), and Wesleyan Methodist Chapels in Middlestown and Netherton.

In addition to providing for the spiritual needs of the parish, the churches and chapels were the focus of much of the social life in the villages. The pages of the Wakefield Express for 1914 describe chapel anniversaries and Sunday School

St Luke's Church and Vicarage

Treats, processions and parades, often led by Netherton Brass Band, concerts and bazaars and many picnics and teas![1]

---

1   Newsome, John *Parish life before the war, 2017* (unpublished)

POPULATION

At the time of 1911 census, the population of the Parish was 3,038, comprising 1,561 males and 1,477 females living in 691 households.

EMPLOYMENT

The main employment was on the land, down the mine, in the mill, the iron foundry or the wood yard.

The area of Shitlington township was 3,380 acres of land and 30 of water (1912 Kelly's Directory of the West Riding of Yorkshire). The major landowners were Viscount Allendale, the Lord of the Manor in Netherton; Lord Savile KCVO; the trustees of George Lane Fox of Bramham; and Sir George Armytage, Bart., of Kirklees Park.

FARMING

The following farmers are listed in Middlestown in 1912: Lister Blakeley; Charles Brook; Edwin Fox; Thomas Killingbeck; Roger Latham; William Mann; Albert Matthews; Joseph Scargill at Smithy Brook and George Smith. Farmers in Netherton were James Barker; Thomas Arthur Beatson; George Bennett of Netherton Hall; Elam Brown; William Charlesworth; Edwin Ellis; George Kilburn of Star Farm; Stringer Brothers; Mrs George Stringer; Fred Walker at Netherton Hall and William Woodcock of Stephenson's Farm. Farmers in Overton were Walter Fretwell, George Hoyland, Albert Morley and Anby Pickles at New Hall Farm. Sam Charlesworth, Richard and Charles Greenwood and Hanson Greenwood of Bank Farm worked the land at Midgley....

MINING

A large proportion of the male population were employed in the local mines at Denby Grange, Caphouse Pit, Prince of Wales and Little London pits, all owned by the Trustees of Miss Lister Kaye. Other colliery owners were Abraham Brooke & Sons Limited and the Flockton Coal Company Limited in Netherton.

EDUCATION

Middlestown mixed and Infants school was erected in 1869 by subscription, at a cost of £1,460 to accommodate 430 children and was enlarged in 1888.

The Headmaster was Sylvester Shackleton and Miss Julia Jarvis was the infants' mistress; the average school attendance in 1912 was 300 children.

Netherton Council School, erected in 1911 to accommodate 270 children, had 200 children on roll and the average attendance (in 1912) was 184. The Headmaster in 1912 was Frank Benning.

Children from the parish attended these schools to the age of 12 years. Some boys were educated at Ossett Grammar School, Wakefield Grammar School and the Wakefield Academy in York Street, Wakefield.

HEALTHCARE

John Arthur Smith MRCS Eng., LSA was the surgeon and medical officer for the Shitlington and Flockton area of Wakefield Union; his house was Stoneleigh, Middlestown.

Herbal and other remedies were advertised in the *Wakefield Express*.

TEXTILES

Thomas Milner, woollen cloth manufacturer, was the proprietor of Coxley Mill.

SHOPS AND SHOPPING

Middlestown Industrial Co-operative Society, manager Byron Todd.

Drapers: Middlestown: Thomas Barker; George Brewer.

Fish fryers: William Metcalf in Middlestown; Joseph Earnshaw in Netherton.

Further supplies would be purchased in Wakefield.

TRANSPORT

The Midland Railway Company had a goods station in the parish; it was situated on the extension line from Royston.

Transport from the parish to other villages and towns would be on foot, by Mrs Armitage's wagonette service, or, very rarely, in one of the few motor cars or lorries available.

Holidays to Blackpool, where 'breezes were still blowing', were advertised in the *Wakefield Express*.

POST OFFICE

William Killingbeck fruiterer and sub postmaster in Middlestown; the letters through Wakefield arrived at 6.45am; letters from the post office were despatched at 6.25pm. There was no Sunday delivery.

Shopkeeper Tom Clarkson was the postmaster in Netherton, where letters through Wakefield arrived at 7.45am and were collected at 2.10pm and 5.55pm on weekdys.

The nearest money order and telegraph office was at Horbury Bridge.

THE HALIFAX BUILDING SOCIETY

The Halifax Building Society was offering reasonable rates of interest on investments:

SPORTS AND PASTIMES

Football, cricket and athletics were major sports in the parish, with knurr and spell being played by some. Many local young men were members of Middlestown Athletic Club and golf was the chosen sport of at least one future soldier.

S(H)ITLINGTON PARISH COUNCIL

Local affairs were overseen by S(h)itlington Parish Council. Several fathers of soldiers, including William Henry Bedford, served as council members. This Parish Council was not the Parochial Church Council, but rather a civil authority set up under the Local Government Act of 1894. The first meeting of Shitlington Parish Council took place in January 1895, with five councillors representing Netherton and six councillors representing Middlestown, under the Chairmanship of Joshua Ingham. (The name 'Sitlington' was adopted in 1929).

Separate from the Parish Council was the Rural District Council, which included a Shitlington Local Committee. The overall local authority was the West Riding County Council.

PUBLIC HOUSES

Public Houses in the parish included the following: at Middlestown, the White Swan and Little Bull, at Overton the Black Swan and the Reindeer, at Midgley the Black Bull

and at Netherton the Bingley Arms and the Star.

Contemporary accounts, including the pages of the *Wakefield Express*, give some information about the lead up to the declaration of war on 4 August 1914, but give little indication of the horror which was to come.

THE HOME
FRONT

Hilary Haigh

THIS CHAPTER WILL look at life for those who stayed behind to look after the families of the men who were fighting and the hardships and difficulties which they suffered. (In a later section will examine the hospitality given in the parish to Belgian families who had escaped to Great Britain when their country was invaded by the German army in August 1914).

The outbreak of war on 4 August 1914 had an immediate effect on local trade. By 8 August 1914, the *Wakefield Express* was reporting that

> …the suspension of trade with the Continent has had a serious effect in Wakefield and district, as many of our most important concerns have extensive dealings with Russia, Germany, France and other foreign countries. This particularly applies to Messrs. E. Green and Son, Ltd., who in normal times always have a large number of men abroad […ing] their world renowned speciality. The worsted and cloth-mills as a rule will be hard hit, but Messrs Colbeck Bros., Ltd., Alverthorpe, who manufacture blue serge and khaki in large quantities for the Government, are working at high pressure, and it is believed the demand for this kind of clothing material will be for a long time greater than the supply. The Walton Pit has been temporarily closed, and other collieries, if they are not closed, must in the immediate future, go on short time, owing to the cessation of shipments from Goole, Hull, and Immingham.

Other preparation for war included the commandeering by the military authorities of assets such as horses:

> During the week military officers, accompanied by veterinary surgeons and armed with the requisite authority, have been riding around in motor-cabs on the look-out for horses suitable for the army. Many useful animals have been obtained in this way. The owners, of course, will be recompensed, although in every instance they stand to lose rather than to gain….in most instances the owners have been sufficiently patriotic to make the sacrifice without grumbling. Mechanical traction has also received attention, and several motor-waggons have been transferred from private owners to the Government.

In August 1914, only three weeks after war was declared, residents of Middlestown were organising themselves, ready to assist the war effort:

> **Middlestown to help the wounded**
>
> With a view to giving practical help in this emergency, a combined meeting, without distinction of sex, creed, or class, has been held in the village. Various forms in which service could be given were discussed. The following officials were elected:- President, Mrs F. H. Waterhouse; Vice President, Mrs S. Shackleton; treasurer, Mrs C. B. Young; secretary, Mrs Geo Ingham; executive committee—Mesdames J.A. Smith, F. Fitton, R.W. Young, J. Hooper, W. Killingbeck, F. Fisher and J. Medlock. Mrs C. B. Young, Overton Lodge, who is taking a deep interest in the scheme, generously gave a tea on Saturday in the beautiful grounds attached to the Lodge, when close upon 400 persons enjoyed the excellent repast… Afterwards an excellent concert was given in the grounds…
>
> *Wakefield Express* 29 August 1914

In the months which followed these ladies arranged first aid classes, the production of knitted socks and other garments as gifts to be supplied to the men at the front, as well as organising the sending of Christmas cards and letters from the village.

The Vice-President was the wife of the Headmaster of St Luke's School, Sylvester Shackleton; they lived in Victoria Cottage.

The Secretary, Mrs Ingham, who was born in Hassop, Derbyshire, was the wife of George Ingham, mining tool manufacturer of Burnbrae Cottage, Middlestown. Isabella and George were the parents of Isabella Black Ingham, John Young Ingham and Charles Robert Ingham; later in the war, Charles Robert Ingham, in civilian life an employee of Ossett Corporation Gas Work, a lieutenant in the West Yorkshire Regiment, was wounded three times and by May 1917 was in hospital in Manchester.

Mrs C. B. Young of Overton Lodge, was the wife of Charles Black Ingham, who was also born in Hassop, Derbyshire and was the brother of Mrs Ingham. (Their mother, Isabella Young, born in Kelso, Roxburghshire, lived in Kelso Cottage).

Support for the troops came in many forms and from men, women and children. Some women worked in the mills and on the farms, others engaged in practical activities to make scarves, socks and shirts to send to the troops, paid for by fund raising events such as whist drives, concerts and house to house collections.

Sponsored by the churches and chapels, working parties were set up in Middlestown/Overton and in Netherton and their activities centred on support for the soldiers and their wives and families as well as the refugees displaced by the war in Europe.

In December 1914 it was reported that The Women Workers' Committee: Hope to be able to send a pair of socks or a belt as a Christmas gift to as many as possible of those who have joined the army and navy from this locality. Gifts of this work should be sent to the Secretary (Mrs Ingham) during the coming week. £2 has been sent to Princess Mary's Fund, of which £1 had been collected by Mr Shackleton from the scholars and teachers of St Luke's Day Schools, and £1 by Mrs Ingham (3s-6d by Master Joshua Ingham aged 4 years). Many subscriptions have been sent up by individuals.

The *Wakefield Express* of 5 December 1914 helpfully advertised 'Useful Presents for our Forces' and the Middlestown and Overton Women Workers' group sent 23 pairs of socks, 11 scarves, 7 belts, 16 pairs of mittens and one helmet. It was also reported that the Committee had in hand 'a good supply of wool for socks and would be glad to get help…'.

On 2 January 1915 the *Wakefield Express* reported as follows:

For Our Gallant Defenders

The Middlestown and Overton women workers have sent out gifts and Xmas cards to the following soldiers now in the army:- Privates A. Thompson, H. Frost, J. Byrom, R. Bedford, M. Dodsworth, E. Schofield, M. Rhodes, W. Parsons, C. Froggatt, W. Fox, C. C. Bedford*, F. Cuff, B. Gascoigne, W. Taylor*, J. A. Littlewood*, W. H. Bedford*, S. Fox, E. Sutcliffe*, B. Howden*, A. Clark, M. Senior, C. Heywood, J. Dunn*, A. Tattersley, T. Saunders*, L. Wiper, L. Belk, E. Bradbury, and W. Hooper*; Drivers H. Howden* and W. Peace; Seamen interned in Holland; Privates W. Lee, T. Townsend, James McCall and J. T. McCall. If by mischance anyone has been overlooked the Secretary (Mrs Ingham) would be glad to hear from relatives, so that a parcel may be forwarded. (* indicates that the name is inscribed on the St Luke's War Memorial)

By March 1915, £64 13s 5d collected in Netherton village had been forwarded to the Wakefield Rural District Distress Committee, which had granted £12 from the fund to be used to give financial relief to the wives of Netherton soldiers.

The same newspaper recorded that the Netherton Working Party, by various efforts, including a tea, concerts, church offertory and private subscriptions, had raised the sum of £20-5s-6d, of which £18-12s-11½d had been spent on making the following garments: 39 shirts, 30 scarves, 26 body-belts, 62 pairs of socks, 2 pairs of mittens, 48 pillow-cases (sent to Clayton Hospital) and 16 handkerchiefs.

This letter published in the *Wakefield Express* of 17 April 1915 indicated the value of these efforts:

1st 4th KOYLI

(To the Editor of the Express)

Sir, on behalf of the officers, non-commissioned officers, and men of the 1st 4th KOYLI, I should like to take this opportunity of thanking all those who have so generously subscribed to the fund for providing socks, shirts, handkerchiefs, and other woollen articles, and also all those who have so willingly helped in the making of these comforts so much needed and appreciated by the men.

The men of the Battalion have already received over 2,000 pairs of socks, about 1.400 shirts, nearly 1,000 mufflers, mittens, and handkerchiefs and body belts where required. They are, therefore, well fitted up for active service, but will need additional supplies sent out from time to time.

Further contributions, either of money or other gifts, will be gratefully acknowledged, and forwarded as required; they should be addressed to my wife, c/o the Depot, 1st 4th KOYLI, Vicarage Street, Wakefield.—Yours etc.

H. J. Haslegrave
Lieut.-Colonel Commanding
1st 4th KOYLI
York April 12th 1915. (17 April 1915 p11)

A more personal response was received from Driver Robert Bentley:

The fortnightly Sisterhood meeting in connexion with the P.M. Chapel took place on Monday…Mrs Kaye presided, and read a letter from Driver Robert Bentley (in France), who had received a parcel from the Sisterhood. He said he was very thankful that the people in the old village still remembered them, as they had been very busy since the big push started in July...The collection raised 5s-10d towards parcels for the boys at the front

Wakefield Express 14 October 1916 p6

In 1916 many local men had been involved in the Battle of the Somme. The government film showing scenes from the battle was shown in local Wakefield cinemas in August 1916:

Wakefield Express 26 August 1916 p8

In collaboration with the YMCA, the *Wakefield Express* launched a scheme to faciliate families exchanging photographs to keep soldiers and their families in touch.

Christmas presents were sent again in December 1916:

Xmas presents. - All soldiers and sailors of Middlestown, Overton and Coxley, numbering 82, serving either at home or abroad, are to receive a Xmas present, consisting of socks, cubes, tinned meat, fruits etc. These are being sent by the Women Workers. The children of St Luke's Schools also intend sending in the same parcel a khaki handkerchief to each soldier as a small memento. The Men's Working Party, along with the members of the WMC and Institute, are also contemplating sending each soldier a gift of tobacco, and already a very good sum of money has been realised for this purpose. A whist-drive and dance is to be held to raise yet more money.

Presents for Soldiers
A meeting of the Distress Committee was held last night week, when it was decided to have an envelope house-to-house collection in aid of Christmas presents for the Netherton soldiers at the front.

Wakefield Express 18 Nov 1916 p6

One year later, the *Wakefield Express* reported that a Whist Drive and Dance promoted by the committee of the Middlestown and Overton Soldiers and Sailors Xmas Parcel Fund had taken place in St Luke's Schoolroom. The President of the Fund, Cr W. Inman, stated that the object of the evening was to enable the committee to 'send all the Overton and Middlestown soldiers a parcel as an Xmas gift from the men of the two villages named, as a reminder that they were ever present in the thoughts of the folk at home…As a result of this effort a profit of over £14 was realised…' (*Wakefield Express* 3 Nov 1917 p8).

The same edition of the newspaper reported good work of the Sisterhood of the Primitive Methodist chapel…'many a lad had been cheered in the trenches by the beautiful letters that had been written, and also by the parcels which had been sent out, [and] many grateful letters had been received…' (*Wakefield Express* 3 Nov 1917 p8)

The same group of ladies were instrumental in organising the accommodation for the group of Belgian refugees, as described in later. The increase in prices affected everyone in the village and this letter published in the *Wakefield Express* in December 1915 tells its own story:

the farmer, in my opinion, is one of the chief instigators of the prices of foodstuffs going up, both English and Colonial, and for your correspondent to say that the English farmer has not been encouraged—well, surely he does not expect the Government to give more than what they are giving him. In respect of team labour advancing 1s per day for man and horse, he contends that horse flesh and horse keep are much dearer. Who is responsible for this but himself? The farmer both breeds the horses and grows the food…In Middlestown there are a few farmers, who have about 30 acres of land, and they each employ a farm labourer, and in the house the wife can afford a maid. Can a colliery worker afford this? No; because the colliery worker, who represents the chief industry in Middlestown, has to pay for higher prices in living, and also to help pay the 1s per day advance to the farmer for team labouring…

Overcharged

Middlestown Dec 8th 1915

From an examination of the 1911 census it is apparent that another cause of local discontent was the overcrowding in many households. The shortage of housing is described in a letter to Sitlington Council printed in the *Wakefield Express* of 26 September 1916:

'SHITLINGTON PARISH COUNCIL AND TOWN PLANNING, ETC

Sir, __ I have read with interest the above Council's discussion re Town Planning. Houses are undobtedly urgently needed in Middlestown and district. But let us have *houses*, for we have too many of the two rooms and a quarter type, ie one living room downstairs (where washing, baking etc has to be carried on, a most unhealthy state of affairs); one bedroom 4 yards square and the other—well, one has to undress on the stairs! While we have this state of affairs we shall always need our isolation hospitals, National Health Commissioners etc. Likewise it is a disgusting state of affairs that young men and young women, on coming home from the pits and mills, should have to wash in full view of the other members of the family. When one wants a bath it means waiting till all the others are off to bed or else turning them into the street. I know plenty of people in Middlestown who would gladly pay reasonable rent for a decent house with proper facilities for having a bath etc and for a place they could call home, and where they could enjoy a quiet evening after the day's work—not a stuffy little place where one feels compelled to go outside to breathe…

Will some members of the Council, who live in decent houses, ask themselves if they would like to live in the common type of house we have here? I am certain the better type of house would pay the landlords equally as well. May Shitlington Parish Council consider this matter, and set an example to the surrounding districts, is the earnest wish of____

Yours, etc.,
INTERESTED
Middlestown, Sept. 26th, 1916

It was not until after the war that some houses were built by the Council, when, in 1921, 'ten blocks of A South houses' were laid out in Old Road, with the instruction to 'erect at once'.

Other houses were privately owned and others were owned and rented out by Middlestown Co-operative Society; these included three cottages at Mount Pleasant, Middlestown and Unity Terrace, next to the Society's No 1 branch in Netherton.

Middlestown Co-operative Society was central to the life of the parish, providing as it did food, clothing, shoes and household goods in its stores in Middlestown and Netherton.

As well as accommodating counters for the purchase of provisions, drapery, footwear and furniture in the main premises, the outbuildings included a bakehouse and slaughterhouse.

The following Co-op employees joined the colours: Fred Bamforth (York and Lancaster); George M. Farrar (KOYLI); Henry Gill (Royal Garrison Artillery); Wilfred Kaye (KOYLI); Wilfred Lewis (Scottish Rifles); Fred Little (Royal Garrison Artillery); George Preston (KOYLI); Oliver Stansfield (Queen's Own Yorkshire Dragoons); William Stringer (Motor Transport, Army Service Corps); Ernest Thomas (Durham Light Infantry); Albert Woollin (KOYLI); Frank G. Binns (Royal Army Medical Corps).

F. Bamforth
Secretary and Cashier

Fred Bamforth was Secretary of Middlestown Co-operative Society; he married Nellie Taylor of Church Villas, Middlestown in March 1916 before joining the army as a 'Derby recruit'.

By 1 November 1915 two members of staff, Fred Little and Wilfred Lewis were with the forces, 'and a weekly allowance was granted to them from the Society's funds during the time they were serving their King and Country'.

Wilfred Kaye, Head Assistant at the Central Stores of Middlestown Co-operative Society was a Signaller in the 1st/4th King's Own Yorkshire Light Infantry and was killed in action on 9 October 1917; he was twenty-eight years old.

At a Special Emergency meeting of the Middlestown Co-operative Society Committee, held on 25 October 1917, the President, Mr H. Hargreaves, moved

That we tender to Mrs Kaye and Family our deepest sympathy in the great loss they have sustained through the death of their son and brother Wilfred Kaye, who was killed in action somewhere in France on or about Oct 12 1917. He was, up to being called upon to join H.M Forces, an employee of this Society for 10 years...'

However, at a meeting of the Co-op committee on 19 November 1917 it was resolved

...that the allowance granted to the late Wilfred Kaye be discontinued after this week

Wilfred Kaye was a violinist 'of considerable promise' and an active member of St Luke's Church, being a server and choir member. His late father had been the caretaker for the church and St Luke's School. Wilfred is remembered in a stained glass window depicting St Wilfred in St Luke's Church, Overton.

The Co-op Committee had decided in 1915 'that all employees joining His Majesty's Forces shall be reinstated on their return' and in 1917 the committee agreed that 'should F. Bamforth accept a position on national service we continue to pay him 10/- per week'.

The Co-op was a major employer in the Parish, but enlistment by male members of staff 'necessitated the inauguration of female assistance in the Grocery Department'. This policy resulted in the employment of women and girls, some as young as 13 years old. For instance, in November 1917 it was reported that Marjorie Leadbetter, 13 years, and Adelaide Woofenden, 13 years, should be engaged as grocery assistants on the Amalgamated Union of Co-operative Employees' scale.

The rates of remuneration for the men serving in the forces was 5s for single men and 10s for married men, rates which compared favourably to serving soldiers from other local Co-ops.

Throughout the War, the Co-op supported local and national appeals for funding; for instance a grant of £25 was early made to the Prince of Wales Fund and 10/6 was contributed to the Royal Albert Institution, Lancaster on 7 September 1914; a donation of £5 was made in support of the Belgian Distress Fund on 28 September 1914 and on 30 May 1917 a contribution of £5 was made to Wakefield and District War Hospital Fund.

Although profits were slightly down on the previous year, the Co-op was clearly continuing to do quite well in 1917 and a dividend of 2/6 (a reduction of 4d) in the pound was declared at the half-yearly annual meeting.

As the war dragged on, it was more difficult to obtain supplies and Middlootown Co operative Industrial Society tried various methods to ensure equal distribution:

NATIONAL RELIEF FUND.

WAKEFIELD AUXILIARY.

We append a coupon which our readers who desire to contribute to the Prince of Wales' National Relief Fund may fill up —no sum too small—and send to the Town-hall, Wakefield.

I enclose £   s.   d. toward

NATIONAL   RELIEF   FUND.

Name...

Address..

....

This coupon should be filled in, and addressed to The Mayor, Town Hall, Wakefield.

Owing to members rushing and buying up any goods which they felt would run short…Various methods were tried with a view to equal distribution, but still there was great dissatisfaction among the members. The principal shortages were sugar, fats of every description (particularly butter), dried fruits, and, later, canned fruits, fish, jams and syrups. An allotment of goods was tried, viz., ½lb of sugar and one jar of jam with each 10s. purchase of general groceries. This plan did not work well at all, so the plan of allowing each household an equal amount of "scarce" commodities was tried. Again, failure was the result, owing to the varying numbers constituting a family, and the many cases where more than one family resided in the house. The next course adopted was that the Manager and Acting Secretary addressed meetings at the Working Men's Club, Middlestown; the Village Institute, Netherton; and at Thornhill Edge, giving details of the Committee's past efforts to serve every member justly, and outlining the proposed scheme for future distribution. Free discussions followed, and useful suggestions were offered, on which the Committee acted. The scheme now introduced was to allow a fixed weight per head for all families of goods which were difficult to obtain, and a census was taken of members' families. The limited success of this system was due to the fact that, unfortunately, some members gave false numbers and members of their families, and thereby caused much difficulty and annoyance to the management.

Shopping cards were introduced later, and continued until the National Government introduced their well-known ration card…

The government's scheme introduced a system of food rationing for certain items. The first item to be rationed was sugar in January 1918, but by the end of April meat, butter, cheese and margarine were added to the list. Some foods were still in short supply even after the war ended, for instance butter remained on ration until 1920.

The minutes of Middlestown Co-operative Society for sub-committee (Rationing) for 6 December 1917 record the following allocations of food:

Resolved
(1)   That butter be rationed according to weight supplied by government
(2)   That lard be ¼lb per head + ¼lb lard sub
(3)   Currants 1lb per family

(4) Cheese ½lb family to 5; 5–8 1lb
(5) Ham and bacon as cheese
(6) Tea 2oz per head
(7) Sugar ½lb per head

Six weeks later, on 31 January 1918, the sub-committee noted:
'that we call attention to food control re our supplies of butter and margarine supplied during this last four weeks & urge them to use every endeavour to increase our supplies seeing that this is a munition and colliery district'

(WYAS, Kirklees KC63/15/9 Rationing sub-committee 31 January 1918)

'…that owing to scarcity of meat supplies we intend having until further notice a supply of fresh fish on Tuesdays and Wednesdays at Government control prices'

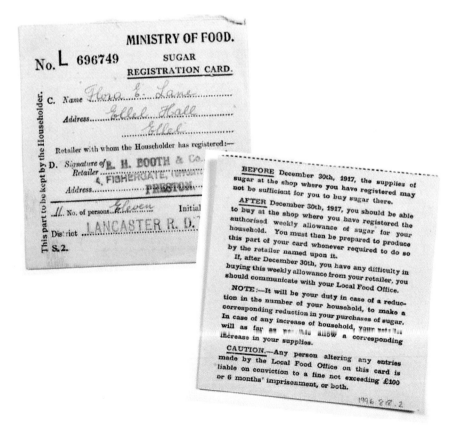

N.E.
164   FOR HOUSEHOLDER'S USE.
SHEFFIELD FOOD CONTROL COMMITTEE.

BUTTER and MARGARINE CARD.

I, (Name of Householder) *Downing*
John
(Address) *49. Brunswick Str.*

having *3* persons in household, desire to purcha
weekly a supply of Butter and Margarine for n
household from
(Name of Shopkeeper) *The Arcade*

(Address of Shop) *Ecclesall Rd*

This card is not transferable and must be produced every tin
Butter and Margarine are purchased. It must be given up
the Householder leaves the City.

The Middlestown Co-operative Society agreed the following rations per family:
Cheese 1lb to 4; 2lb 5-8; 3lb over 8
Currants 1lb per family
Lard ¼lb Head of the Family
Tea 2oz per head
Sugar 1lb
Butter, bacon, ham and margarine to be kept back until we receive
further supplies; also Swiss milk and Lyles' syrup

By the end of the war many families on the Home Front had suffered the
loss or wounding of one of its members. Many young wives had become widows,
mothers had lost sons and children had lost fathers, uncles, brothers or cousins.

Life on the Home Front, although comparatively safe, had been subject to
many hardships, including food shortages and rationing, overcrowding and
housing shortages.

The men who returned would find that the war had changed life in the parish
for everyone and forever.

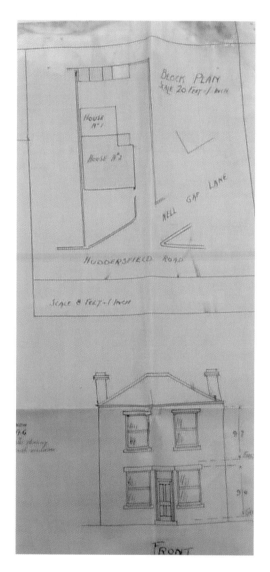

Middlestown Parish Rooms,
accommodation for Belgian refugees

BELGIAN REFUGEES AND THE LOCAL HISTORY OF THE GREAT WAR IN BRITAIN

Dr Rebecca Gill
(University of Huddersfield)

OVER THE COURSE of these centenary years, community historians are beginning to piece together the forgotten story of the reception of Belgian refugees in the towns and villages of Britain during the First World War. The British government's initially ad hoc, but increasingly proficient, administration of the Belgians' dispersal and maintenance has been documented by Peter Cahalan in his book *Belgian Refugee Relief in England in the Great War* (1982), but the local history of their accommodation and day-to-day life in family homes, workplaces and neighbourhoods has, until recently, remained hidden from view. This is not an easy history to uncover and an amount of detective work is required to find traces of Belgian refugees in our local communities. The lived experience of the Belgians themselves is often beyond reach, though snippets of interviews with local newspapers do give a glimpse of their perilous journeys to safety from the Belgian ports to Folkestone and then on to London, before being matched with offers of accommodation from across the British Isles. More accessible, however, are the records of local government and local labour organisations, and these provide an insight into the logistics of their allocation and negotiations around their taking up of paid work. The history of the Belgians' flight is not something with a high profile in Belgium itself and it is interesting to speculate why this might be the case. Belgians with whom I've corresponded, whose own family members were discovered to have been refugees in Britain, were surprised to unearth these stories – family history, they said, was not a particularly popular activity, unlike in Britain. Perhaps the stories of the occupation and suffering of the Second World War have cast longer shadows. Or perhaps as Peter Cahalan has suggested, the flight of some Belgians was felt to be a form of desertion, leaving others to bear the brunt of the Germans' heavy-handed, and in some cases brutal, occupation of their country (this may have been compounded by the fact that the term 'refugee' was also applied to civilians who were directly recruited by French and British manufacturers to shore up depleted supplies of labour for their factories). Certainly, after the war, the Belgian government did not seek to officially commemorate the refugees' plight, possibly in an attempt to heal the wounds of a shattered and already divided country. This has meant that, until now, the local history of the Belgian refugees has remained untold, not just in Britain, where the history of the Western Front has dominated, but also in Belgium.

Initially, the care of the Belgians had been taken up by a voluntary agency (the War Refugees Committee, based in central London), but the Local Government Board stepped in once it became apparent that the numbers seeking sanctuary would quickly overwhelm voluntary efforts. In total, 250,000 Belgians would arrive in Britain, some wealthy enough to pay for their own maintenance (and observed by Virginia Woolf frequenting fashionable parties in the rich boroughs of London), others looked after for the duration of the war by local charities and parishes, and others granted a stipend, and later, the right to work. News of the Belgians' plight filled the national and local press from the early days of the war, when German troops had invaded Belgium in their attempt to reach Paris, and had terrorised the Belgian population through acts of destruction, pillage and summary execution. Belgians detailed their horrifying experiences to local journalists, for example, a M. and Mme. Boxein, who arrived in Slaithwaite in Huddersfield in November 1914, described how,

> Their little farm was occupied by the Huns, who proceeded to burn it, stick, stock, and barrel, so to say. This act of savagery was uncalled for. The occupants were non-combatants, and according to all the laws of war should have been exempt from spoliation and violence. Understand this: they burnt the horses and cattle alive. and terrorised the defenceless people by threatening to shoot them.[1]

---

1   *Colne Valley Guardian*, 27 November, 1914.

Belgian atrocity propaganda – some of it based on fact, some of it, such as reports of babies' hands being chopped off, the product of journalists' colourful fancy - permeated the early days of the war and was a major driver of recruitment initiatives – posters abounded which warned of 'the hun at the door' and stoked fears of a German invasion of Britain. These propaganda images had seeped into the popular imagination to the extent that the government had subsequently to stipulate that most Belgians would be arriving in extended family groups, and that orphans were not going to be available for adoption in any number. Yet these stories were also the spur to a huge wave of compassion and solidarity with the Belgians, which manifested themselves in offers to donate clothing, house Belgian families, pay in to subscription funds, and attend charity fundraisers. Many Belgians were greeted by official welcomes by the local mayor, and crowds of onlookers.

To co-ordinate the numbers of Belgians arriving in the autumn of 1914 with offers of assistance, the Local Government Board requested that the county councils each establish a Belgian Refugee Relief committee, and that it in turn request that local councils did the same. Wakefield, as a county town, was one of the hubs of provision for Belgian refugees. Correspondence preserved in the West Yorkshire Archive Service between the Local Government Board and County Hall in Wakefield show how, as elsewhere, refugee relief was undertaken as a sub-committee of the existing War Distress Committee, which itself had been established at the beginning of the war in expectation of civilian distress in the face of the anticipated slump in the economy (this slump never materialised however, and in most localities the Distress Fund lay dormant). Of the ten individuals whose names are recorded as having sat on the Wakefield "War Refugees Sub-Committee", five were women. This is instructive, for it points to the incorporation of (usually middle-class) women into local government, a feature replicated on other local government committees devoted to welfare during the war, and in the plethora of wartime voluntary bodies concerned with the care of injured troops and the families of serving men, some of which also aided the Belgians.[2]

---

[2]   The "War Refugees Sub-Committee" was chaired by H. Dunn, and had the following members: Mrs Agnes Cross, Mrs L. Milnes Gaskell, Rev. Canon Phipps, Miss Hermione Unwin, G. Saville, T. Snowden, Miss Julia Thornton, The Lady Catherine Milnes Gaskell, Sir John C. Horsfall, Bart.

Care for the needy, was, of course, considered a traditional feminine preserve, but women's work for local government during the war was also a significant recognition of their administrative capabilities at a time when women's suitability for political representation and candidature was so prominently to the fore. A notice in the *Wakefield Express* in January 1915, was typical in its recording of women's labours, particularly in sewing and knitting:

FOR THE BELGIANS—Goods have been sent from Middlestown and Overton to the British Consul in London as follows:- 1 boy's suit, 2 pairs trousers, 14 pairs knickers, 18 petticoats, 4 nightdresses, 2 shirts, 6 pairs stockings, 2 caps, 2 bonnets, 1 scarf. An acknowledgement has been received from Mrs A. B. Balfour, who writes:-'On behalf of the Belgian Minister in London, I beg to thank the Middlestown and Overton women-workers for their parcel received here (per Mrs. G. Ingham) for the Belgian children...'[3]

By February 1915, 2187 Belgians had been found accommodation in the county.[4] Having been despatched on the train from London, where many had been housed temporarily in Alexandra Palace, to Wakefield, the majority were housed locally in properties given for the purpose by local corporations, industrialists or churches. The *Wakefield Express* reported their arrival into Middlestown; they included a number from Antwerp and its environs, following the fall of Antwerp in October 1914:

On Tuesday evening four refugees arrived at Middlestown, and are being housed in the Parish-room, which has been very comfortably furnished. These refugees are Frederic Andre, of Flanders, late of Rue du Sabot, Paris, teacher of French; Theophla Muck, 32 years, Duffel, Belgium, with Philomene Muck, 24 years, his wife, and Frances, their daughter, aged 10 weeks. Muck was a foreman at a paper mill. A further batch arrived on Thursday afternoon. The names are Mr., Mrs., and Master De Vos, from Antwerp.[5]

---

3   *Wakefield Express*, January 1915, p. 16.
4   Minutes, War Refugees Sub-Committee, County Hall, Wakefield, 3 February 1915, West Yorkshire Archive Service, Kirklees, S/ NUDBTW 10.
5   *Wakefield Express*, 12 December 1914, p. 4.

Initially the Belgians were forbidden from working, for fear of antagonising industrial relations at a time of predicted slump in trade and industry and thus charitable endeavours were undertaken to support the Belgians and express solidarity with their plight, and the government provided an allowance. As the following report suggests, however, public donations soon dwindled, no doubt compounded by the steep rise in the cost of living, and the need for families to attend to their own welfare:

> A concert in aid of the Middlestown and Overton Belgian Relief Fund, was given on Monday evening by the Overton Primitive Sunday scholars. A good selection of action songs, war songs, dialogues, recitations etc was given. Mr R.P. Leather, a member of the committee, expressed the thanks of the committee to Misses Emily Waring and Ann Parker, to whom great credit was due for the able manner in which the children had been trained. Miss Waring also recited "In the Pit of Death" and "The Fireman's Wedding". Miss Matilda Verschotten, a refugee, gave a song, for which she was recalled. Miss Parker accompanied all the singing on the harp. There was only a moderate audience. The collection netted £1-6s.[6]

However, once the local economy picked up, Belgians were granted the right to work provided they did not undercut union rates. This, of course, was an important point for the Trade Union movement, which debated the issue at length in the local Trades and Labour Councils. Demand for labour was so strong however, particularly in the local textile industry (the region produced army cloth by the mile during the war) that local manufacturers began to directly recruit Belgians, especially for night shifts in the mills.[7] Belgians were also recruited to work in munitions, though this is an aspect of their history even harder to trace given the wartime censorship surrounding the location of munitions factories. The region did have a number of such factories however, including in Leeds, Huddersfield and Bradford, at which Belgians were employed. The government also established munitions plants staffed entirely by Belgian refugees, such as those

6   *Huddersfield Express*, 17 April 1915 p 4
7   Rebecca Gill, "Brave Little Belgium' arrives in Huddersfield … voluntary action, local politics and the history of international relief work', *Immigrants and Minorities*, 34:2, 132-150.

at Richmond-Twickenham, Letchworth and Birtley (the Armstrong-Whitworth factory in Birtley was staffed entirely by rehabilitated Belgian soldiers). This is a history which is now coming to light through the research of Christophe Declercq and Helen Baker, who have researched the community of Belgians who lived in 'the Belgian village on the Thames' in Richmond-Twickenham and worked at the Pelabon Factory producing shells and gun parts; by July 1917 the Pelabon Factory employed 1705 Belgians.[8]

At the end of the war, the government moved quickly to repatriate the Belgians, fearing hostility from returning British soldiers over the question of their employment. Most had returned by early 1919. Though their residency in Britain was never officially commemorated, or formed a part of the traditional histories of the war which have concentrated on military campaigns and the soldiers' war, the Belgians marked their stay with gifts of gratitude to their former hosts, some of which can still be seen in the region today in the form of plaques and commemorative stone tablets, such as those which adorn the Mechanics Institute in Marsden and the clock tower in Otley marketplace. Some maintained relationships with former neighbours, who paid reciprocal visits in the years following the war, including the aforementioned Boxein family who had resided in Slaithwaite. Investigating the reception of Belgians into our communities can help us better understand the various ways in which the war was experienced in different locales: local politics, women's greater involvement in local government, voluntary traditions and labour relations all influenced the nature of the Belgians' welcome. Their presence in British neighbourhoods thus requires careful research if we are to fully appreciate the texture of home front life during the Great War.

---

8   Christophe Declercq and Helen Baker, 'The Pelabon Munitions works and the Belgian village on the Thames: community and forgetfulness in outer-metropolitan suburbs', *Immigrants and Minorities*, 34: 2, 151-170.

CONSCIENTIOUS OBJECTORS IN BRITAIN DURING THE FIRST WORLD WAR

Cyril Pearce
(University of Leeds)

THE PROCESS OF marking the centenary of the First World War will, inevitably and understandably, concentrate on the business of fighting and its consequences both for the individual combatants and for the societies mobilised to sustain them. There will also be the question of how those societies responded. Was the war necessary? Was it even popular and if popular, for how long? Inherent in these latter questions is the matter of the war's opponents.

For much of the summer of 1914 the attention of the British press and, probably, the British public was pre-occupied with affairs at home; and there was a great deal to be pre-occupied with. Not least the threat of an army mutiny over home rule for Ireland and the increasing militarisation of both Nationalist and Loyalist organisations. The assassination of the heir to the throne of the Austro-Hungarian empire, the Archduke Franz Ferdinand and his wife, on the 28th June, in Sarajevo, was, for a time, little more than another item of bad news from abroad. It was not until the Austro-Hungarian ultimatum to Serbia on the 23rd July that the pre-occupation began to shift. The bustle of diplomatic activity and the preparations for war in Europe posed the question of British involvement. Were there secret treaty obligations which would draw Britain into a war or could she remain aloof as she had done since Waterloo, almost a hundred years earlier? By the August Bank Holiday weekend the sense of what was might happen began to provoke anguished and desperate reactions. A huge public meeting in Trafalgar Square on Sunday the 2 August, organised by the

Labour Party and supported by radical opinion of all kinds, passed a resolution opposing Britain's entry into a European war. That weekend across the country in towns and villages there were meetings organised by churches, women's groups and political organisations, mostly from radical Liberals leftwards to Marxists Socialists, demanding the same thing. All to no avail, on the 4th August Britain entered the war by declaring war on Germany.

Within weeks of the declaration of war, many of those who had been keen to avoid it accepted the situation as their patriotic duty and threw in their lot with the war effort. Many did not. Among them were groups and individuals who had opposed the Boer War, the arms race of the pre-war years and the National Service League's campaign to introduce conscription for Britain's young men. Most of them were drawn from existing political organisations. Of these the socialist Independent Labour Party (ILP), the major political group within the Parliamentary Labour Party, was probably the most important. Also from the political 'Left' were Anarchists, elements of the British Socialist Party (BSP), the Socialist Labour Party (SLP) and the Socialist Party of Great Britain (SPGB). Arguments opposing the war from these 'political' war resisters ranged from the essentially moral and humanitarian views of a great many ILP and Socialist Sunday School members to the more overtly class conscious view that the war was a war for foreign markets and empire and had nothing to do with working men and women.

The anti-war cause was not an entirely socialist or 'Leftist' movement. It did include people from other parts of the political spectrum. Radical Liberalism was thrown into disarray by the war and many of its local adherents left the party to join the anti-war movement and, in some cases, eventually to join the Labour Party. The women's movement was also divided. Emmeline Pankhurst and her daughter Christabel declared an end to militancy and tried to lead the members of the Women's Social and Political Union (WSPU), the 'Suffragettes', into support for the war. Not all the WSPU's grass-root militants were convinced and, epitomised by the other Pankhurst daughters, Sylvia and Adela, opposed the war.

Opposition to the war was not simply a political matter. For many Christians and some Jews, the 6th Commandment, 'Thou shalt not kill', took precedence over patriotic duty. Notwithstanding the theological sophistry of the 'Just war' they opposed the war and, when it came to it, refused to take up arms. Chief among them was the Society of Friends, the Quakers. Although at least a third of all eligible Quaker men joined the armed forces, the rest did not. Instead they chose other forms of service or, as conscientious objectors, no war service at all. Other nonconformist sects joined those who refused to fight although not all of them could be said to have been part of the anti-war movement. Christadelphians, International Bible Students (later Jehovah's Witnesses), Plymouth Brethren, 7th Day Adventists and others rejected this particular call of the state although their view of themselves as part of God's Kingdom on earth prevented them from joining with other 'political' war resisters. While these particular sects can be said to have opposed the war, individual members of most of the main Christian denominations were to be found among the war resisters, from Roman Catholics and Anglicans, through Wesleyan Methodists to Congregationalists and Primitive Methodists. The difference was that, in many cases, the leadership of these denominations either, as in the case of the Church of England, took a pro-war stance or refused to take a stand at all on the grounds that to do so would divide the faithful. In the case of Roman Catholics or Jews there was an understandable reluctance to have accusations of lack of patriotism attached to an already toxic brew of anti-Irish or anti-semitic prejudice.

At the beginning, the business of opposing the war was largely about propaganda, but propaganda in an increasingly hostile environment. As casualties mounted and the war dragged on into 1915, reactions to the apparently disloyal or openly un-patriotic anti-war movement became unpredictable and at times violent. Holding public anti-war meetings in the open air or indoors became difficult. Some were attacked and anti-war campaigners assaulted. The possibility of this kind of violence prompted local authorities to ban public open-air meetings and to deny them the use of civic buildings and school halls. It also encouraged the owners of theatres and private assembly rooms to do the same. Writing to the press was also constrained and press self-censorship reduced the amount of coverage for anti-war views. It was, however, the introduction of the Defence of the Realm Act in 1914, which most hampered the anti-war cause. Its clauses which made it an offence to make a speech or to publish writing likely to cause disaffection or to discourage recruiting, although not rigorously applied, did make campaigning fraught with difficulty. Nevertheless, campaigning against the war persisted.

The actual stand made by young men of military service age varied enormously. For some, while they refused to take up arms, there was a humanitarian imperative that they help the wounded and support the war's refugees. This applied from the very beginning of the war. The best known examples are the Friends' Ambulance Unit (FAU) and the Friends' War Victims Relief Service (FWVRS) which were formed in the early months of the war. By 1918 they had involved almost two thousand men and women in humanitarian work throughout the European theatre of war. What is less well-known is that until 1916 many young men volunteered to serve in a non-combatant capacity in the Royal Army Medical Corps (RAMC) or the Royal Army Service Corps (RASC). Their understanding that they would be treated as non-combatants only became more generally known when, in 1918, the Army High Command decided to transfer them to combatant units and they resisted, in many cases to the point of Court Martial and prison. In purely legal terms these humanitarian volunteers were not 'Conscientious Objectors' not because of their volunteering but because they did so before the introduction of Conscription.

Until 1916, alone among the combatant nations, Britain did not have compulsory military service. However, faced by the war's apparently insatiable appetite for more and more men, Asquith's Liberal government gave in to pressure and in January 1916 approved the first Military Service Act and in so doing introduced Britain, for the first time, to the idea of compulsory military service. This required military service by all single men from England, Scotland and Wales between the ages of 18 and 40. Given the very real political and security issues there, conscription was not applied in Ireland. In May 1916 further legislation extended conscription to married men and by 1918 the net had been spread even wider to include fifty-year olds. The legislation allowed conscripts the opportunity to appeal to a local Tribunal to defer or even suspend their call-up. The Tribunal were to consider seven acceptable grounds for some sort of exemption including domestic hardship, the need to complete their education, illness, business, or the national importance or war-essential nature of their work. These were listed 'a' to 'g'. It was the addition of the 'conscience clause', clause 'f' which created 'Conscientious Objectors' (COs). Men who were not prepared to serve as combatants were allowed to apply for exemption from service on grounds of conscience. The anti-war movement interpreted that as meaning COs could be granted Absolute Exemption from war service of any kind. The government and the Tribunal system took a different view by allowing COs exemption only from combatant service.

The introduction of conscription proved to have a very mixed effect on the anti-war movement. For the first time in the war it meant that the movement's men of military service age had to decide how best to express their opposition to the war. It was no longer simply a matter of refusing to volunteer, the arrival of their call-up papers demanded a response. The working of the conscription process had other effects. On the one hand, one way or another, it removed male anti-war activists from both local and national campaigns – although, in doing so it created gaps which were ably filled by the anti-war movement's women. On the other hand, the imprisonment of COs, their sometimes brutal treatment and the local contest between COs and authority which characterised most Tribunal proceedings created moments of 'theatre' and an almost inexhaustible supply of news-worthy stories from which the anti-war movement in all its forms derived stories of 'heroic' resistance and from which it drew a measure of solidarity which, at times, it had seemed to lack.

The Military Service Tribunal structures were in place from January 1916 to November 1918. During the whole of that time COs came before them to plead their cause. What drove them to this point of the public declaration of their views varied as did the course of action they were prepared to take. Of the 20,000 COs who can be identified appearing before the Tribunals, the vast majority, perhaps 14,000 were prepared to offer some sort of service short of carrying and using arms. Many whose work was regarded as being either essential to the war effort of to maintaining the fabric of society and its economy were allowed to remain in their existing occupations. Others, prepared to do work of national importance which was not directly war-related and not under military control were found work on the land or in essential service industries. Some, like the pre-conscription non-combatant volunteers, were enlisted in the RAMC and more than 3,000 agreed to serve in the specially created Non-Combatant Corps (NCC).

For the 6,000 or more who were prepared to do none of these things the route was very different. Their appeals for exemption were refused and they were handed over to the military. At this point some gave in and accepted army discipline; the majority did not. The next step for them was a Court Martial for disobedience and a sentence to time, usually 112 days with hard labour, in a civil prison. But this was not always the case. In May and June of 1916 the Army's response was to send thirty-five COs to France. There their refusal to obey orders was a capital offence. They were sentenced to death by firing squad. It is not clear whether in doing this the Army was hoping to make examples of COs to discourage the rest but the government had a very different view. The executions did not go ahead and the sentences were commuted to ten years' penal servitude.

For about 1,500 'Absolutists' who would have nothing to do with any schemes or palliatives, the rest of the war was spent going from prison to Court Martial and back to prison again. A number of COs had as many as five Courts Martial. This obdurate group also supplied the COs who refused prison work and those who went on hunger strike and were force-fed.

In August 1916, for those Court Martialled and imprisoned at least once, there was the Home Office Scheme (HOS). This was centred on work of national importance which was not in any way war-related. The Absolutists refused it arguing that any work in wartime was, in some way, war-related. Those who accepted the scheme, the 'Alternativists' disagreed. This division was one of the first major ruptures in the previously united front the COs had presented.

For a time these schemes were called 'settlements' which suggested a purpose which was rather more positive than the reality. One of the earliest of them, digging roadstone in quarries at Dyce, near Aberdeen, was a short-lived and almost disastrous embarrassment. From August until October 1916 more than 250 men were sent there. Some of them were 'Frenchmen' who had been repatriated to English prisons from army custody in France, mostly to Winchester. Others who the Central Tribunal deemed to be genuine COs and who, at first, appeared to have accepted the Home Office Scheme joined them from prisons across the country. Accommodation was in reject leaky army tents on a wet site which Aberdeenshire's September rains soon made a quagmire. Food was inadequate and the work beyond the ability of many of the men newly-released from prison and, in some cases, punishment diets. On the 8th September Walter Roberts, an ILP man from Stockport, died after a high fever and a short illness. Thereafter work at the camp became difficult. Men refused to work more than five hours a day and some rejected the Scheme altogether.

After this death and near-rebellion, rather more care was taken in selecting and managing the Scheme. HOS men were eventually kept in a number of empty prisons – Wakefield, Warwick, Dartmoor and Knutsford – and in work camps on forestry, quarrying and other schemes in different parts of the country. In the former prisons, while much of the work was normal prison work, the cells were not locked, neither COs nor warders were in uniform, and the centres were allowed a measure of self-regulation.

The whole of this structure remained in place until the spring of 1919 when the Absolutists were released from prison and the men on the HOS and on work of national importance away from home were gradually allowed to return to civilian life.

Drawing together the different sections of the anti-war movement, co-ordinating its campaigns and supporting the COs and their families, were a number of organisations which functioned at both local and national levels. The ILP and, after 1916, the BSP, were the only main-stream and substantial political organisations which were committed to the anti-war cause. In both cases, local branches and a good many individual members, took different lines but the national party line remained firmly opposed to the war and to conscription. The same is true of the Society of Friends. Its Friends' Service Committee became an important part of the anti-war movement. However, it was three other organisations, largely created by the war and the desire to resist conscription, which drew much of the movement together and helped give it a national voice – the Fellowship of Reconciliation (FOR), the Union of Democratic Control (UDC) and the No-Conscription Fellowship (NCF). Minority left-wing fragments all opposed to the war, such as Anarchists, the SPBG and the SLP, added to the numbers and their individual members were often highly influential, although their national presence was insubstantial.

The FOR grew from an initiative within the Society of Friends in August 1914. It was an essentially Christian and pacifist organisation which saw its members taking part in the 'Ministry of Reconciliation between man and man, class and class, nation and nation'. As such it was a campaigning, even evangelical, but determinedly non-political organisation.

If the FOR campaigned for 'reconciliation' then the UDC was rather more specific. Its central concern was that the war had come about as a consequence of the lack of democratic accountability in the making of British foreign policy. Coming together shortly after the outbreak of war, the UDC was, in effect, a combination of the war's critics drawn initially from the Liberal party but also involving members of the ILP. It was the brain-child of Charles Trevelyan, Liberal MP for Elland in the West Riding, a junior minister in Asquith's Liberal government who had resigned his post at the outbreak of war. He was joined by Arthur Ponsonby, also a Liberal MP and former private secretary to the Liberal Prime Minister, Henry Campbell-Bannerman. E. D. Morel, a campaigning journalist, who had resigned his membership of the Liberal party, became UDC secretary and treasurer. By the spring of 1915 the UDC's executive committee had also recruited senior figures from the ILP in Ramsay MacDonald MP, Philip Snowden MP. It was not a pacifist organisation and, despite the participation of senior Socialists, had no analysis based on notions of the war as a product of the competition for empire or the failings of international capitalism. Fenner Brockway described its leaders as 'bourgeois to their fingertips' so much so that ' … they might have been lifted out of any gathering of the gentlemen of England …' Nevertheless, its Manifesto, published in November 1914 established a number of the points of principle which, it hoped, would pave the way for the democratic control of foreign policy and create guarantees of peace. However, the process could only begin with an early settlement of the war according to four cardinal principles:

- The principle of self- determination.
- The ratification of treaties by Parliament.
- The abandonment of the 'balance of power principle' and its replacement by the idea of the 'concert of nations' which would set up an international council and the machinery to guarantee peace.
- Multi-lateral disarmament and the nationalisation of the arms industry.

The idea of an early negotiated settlement and the beginnings of a post-war system to guarantee peace was its major contribution to the wartime debate. The political seniority of its major members and supporters gave the anti war cause articulate and talented advocates at the highest levels of British Parliamentary democracy. The UDC's campaigning pamphlets were important statements of its policy and helped sustain the criticism of the war and to establish its Manifesto as a basis for the construction of a lasting peace. Its monthly journal, *The UDC*, reinforced its pamphlets campaigns by including articles written by its leading members which were both policy statements and commentaries on the war.

Beyond all that, it had a local presence in the form of more than a hundred branches spread across the country and a monthly journal which reported their activities. It was *The UDC* which by reporting on branch activity helped sustain a sense of the UDC as not simply an elite metropolitan organisation. For example, *The UDC* issue for December 1916, carried the following report of its Birmingham branch's activities in November.

> **Birmingham**: The following meetings have been addressed by our speakers during November: Sparkhill Women's Co-operative Guild, by Rev. Morgan Whiteman; Handsworth Women's Co-operative Guild by Councillor Harrison Barrow; Amalgamated Society of Carpenters and Joiners by Mr J. E. Southall; Operative Bricklayers' Society by Mr E. W. Hampton; No.10 branch N.U.R. by Mr W. Milner; Bournville Women's Co-operative Guild, by Rev. Morgan Whiteman; Railway Clerks' Association by Councillor J. W. Kneeshaw; Bristol Street Adult School Class XIV by Councillor Harrison Barrow. Owing to the exigencies of the Military Service Act, our Organiser, Mr Fred Longden is no longer with us, but is awaiting sentence of Court Martial. Our Treasurer has also left to take up alternative service offered him by the Tribunal. Please address all communications to the Secretary, Hubert W. Lemon at 69, Mostyn Road, Handsworth, Birmingham.

Such reports from as far afield as Yeovil in Somerset and both Edinburgh and Glasgow in Scotland, give a sense of the UDC's reach and of the difficulties faced by those of its members who were of military service age.

It was arguably the NCF which proved to be the dominant factor within the anti-war movement. From the very beginning of the war there were those who felt that it was unlikely that the British war effort would be sustained by an entirely volunteer army and that conscription would soon replace voluntarism. For those within the anti-war movement this, as much as the war itself, was to be resisted. One form of opposition began as an idea launched by Fenner Brockway, who, at the outbreak of war was editor of the ILP's newspaper the *Labour Leader*.

In November 1914, he published an appeal inviting all young men who intended to refuse military service, to join a 'No-Conscription Fellowship'. The response was encouraging. By February 1915 the NCF had 339 members and the names of a number of men beyond military service age who were prepared to help. Originally organised by Fenner Brockway and his wife Lilla from their house in Derbyshire, the flow of new members and its developing work prompted the opening of a head office in London later that summer.

By that time the British system of voluntary recruitment was in trouble. The Derby Scheme, which attempted to encourage every man of military age to 'attest' his willingness to serve should he be called on to do so, was voluntarism's last throw and it failed. By late autumn conscription seemed inevitable. As a consequence, membership of the NCF grew to the point where it became necessary to convene its first national conference. This was held in London in November against a background of press hostility and attempts to disrupt proceedings by groups of soldiers and pro-war civilians.

The conference formally agreed the NCF's organisation, elected its National Committee and set down its definition of the 'Statement of Faith' as the basis of membership.

The No-Conscription Fellowship is an organisation of men likely to be called up for military service in the event of conscription, who will refuse from conscientious motives to bear arms, because they consider human life to be sacred, and cannot, therefore, assume the responsibility of inflicting death. They deny the right of Governments to say. 'You shall bear arms,' and will oppose every effort to introduce compulsory military service into Great Britain. Should such efforts be successful, they will, whatever the consequences may be, obey their conscientious convictions rather than the commands of Governments.

Within three months of the NCF's inaugural national conference and its declaration of principle, conscription had been introduced with the first Military Service Act. At the beginning of March when the first COs were beginning to appear before local Tribunals to plead their cases, the NCF launched its weekly newspaper, *The Tribunal*. Despite police raids and attempts to close it down, it continued in print until it was closed-down voluntarily in January 1920.

Although unquestionably the most significant, the NCF was not the only anti-war grouping in Britain during the 1914-18 war. Its commitment to 'oppose every effort to introduce compulsory military service' had already been the major part of its work for much of the summer of 1915. In this it was joined by other organisations from within the broad anti-war community which came together in a broad and hectic campaign largely co-ordinated by the National Council Against Conscription, later the National Council for Civil Liberties (NCCL) to prevent the inevitable introduction of the first Military Service Bill. This eleventh hour attempt to co-ordinate resistance, came too late. However, something of that failed campaign was preserved in the creation of the Joint Advisory Council – better known as the 'JAC'. This co-ordinated the work of three principal anti-war groups; the NCF, the Fellowship of Reconciliation and the Friends' Service Committee (FSC) for the remainder of the war years and beyond.

One of the JAC's principal activities became known as the Conscientious Objector Information Bureau (COIB). Using mostly NCF branches and a national networks of volunteer supporters it gathered data about CO experiences – Tribunal hearings, Courts Martial, prison, Home Office Scheme. It also liaised closely with Quaker prison visitors and chaplains. Data gathered in this way was used to inform on-going debates in Parliament about the treatment of COs. Sympathetic MPs, Philip Snowden (Labour) and Ted Harvey (Liberal) amongst them, were primed with evidence for Parliamentary questions and Catherine Marshall, the NCF's political secretary, used every opportunity to keep the anti-war debate alive. To help with this from March 1916 until the spring of 1919, the COIB published a weekly Report. The Report was cyclostyled and circulated first to NCF branches and to the editor of *The Tribunal*. There it was used as the basis for the lists of COs and their experiences published throughout 1916 and as copy for articles as issues arose. It was also sent to more than 200 men and women from within the broader anti-war community and to others who were regarded as opinion-formers whose sympathy might be helpful.

Supporting this 'national' presence was the activity of the anti-war movement's local branches. At this level branches of the NCF joined with the local FOR, the ILP and elements of the BSP to form their own No-Conscription Councils also known as local branches of the National Council for Civil Liberties (NCCL). Local Quaker meetings, Adult Schools, trade unions and individuals were also represented. The work of the local NCF and the NCCL branches was essentially about three things. First, to continue the anti-war campaign by leafleting, holding meetings and writing to the press. Second, by supporting COs and reporting on their experiences within the system. Classes for COs were held to help them in making their case before the Tribunals. Tribunal hearings were monitored by 'watchers' and, once the CO was in the system, reports were sent back to the branch so that his family might be informed. Thirdly, it was about fund-raising. The money was to sustain the organisation, locally and nationally, but it was also to help support COs' families who were in difficulties.

A selective memory wishing to belittle the efforts of the anti-war movement would prefer to suggest that its people and their struggles were only evident and indeed, only relevant, in wartime. There are even those who would dismiss COs and their supporters as 'Cranks'. That was far from the case. The anti-war struggle had far-reaching effects on British politics, not least on the Liberal party many of whose members left to join Labour. Within the Labour party, the anti-war activists, men and women, continued to play key roles in the party in the inter-war years and beyond. Many became local Councillors and some, Members of Parliament. The Society of Friends, with the majority of the pro-war Quakers gone and new members drawn from other 'religious' anti-war men and women, emerged in the post-war world more committed to its traditional pacifist stance than before. From the campaign to resist the passing of the Military Service Acts came the National Council of Civil Liberties. It remains a resilient defender of the rights of conscience a hundred years later in the form of 'Liberty'. The peace movements of the post-war world also owed much to the personnel who had worked for the NCF, the UDC or the FOR. Indeed, some of the founder-members of the Campaign for Nuclear Disarmament in the 1950s were former First World War COs. The imprint of the struggle for peace is not confined to the years 1914 to 1918, nor even to the rest of the twentieth century. It continues to have its reverberations as we consider the centenary of that hideous slaughter.

SCHOOL
LIFE

St Luke's School, Middlestown WYAS, Wakefield WYW1547/25

MIDDLESTOWN SCHOOL IN THE FIRST WORLD WAR

Hilary Haigh

ST LUKE'S SCHOOL was located on New Road, near the junction with Nell Gap Lane and adjacent to St Luke's Church.

BACKGROUND HISTORY

LOCATION
The staff and pupils at Middlestown School were not shielded from the effects of war. Fathers, brothers, uncles and cousins were in the forces and staff were called upon to fight themselves or support their husbands as they went to war.

The school was very much involved with fund raising and the production of Christmas presents for the men at the front, as the following extracts from the school log book bear witness.[1]

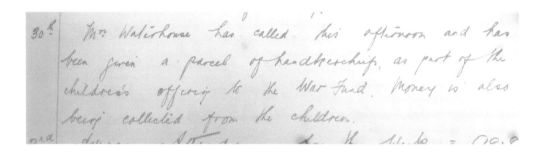

30 September 1914 Mrs Waterhouse[2] has called this afternoon and has been given a parcel of handkerchiefs as part of the children's offering to the War Fund. Money is also being collected by the children.

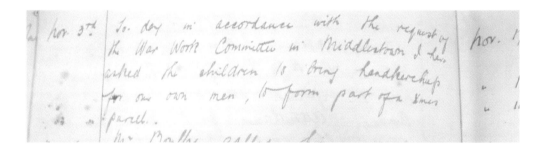

3 November 1915 Today in accordance with the request of the War Work Committee in Middlestown I have asked the children to bring handkerchiefs for our own men, to form part of an Xmas parcel.

1   WYAS, Wakefield St Luke's school log book WMD4/2/25/1
2   Mrs Waterhouse was Chairman of the War Work Committee

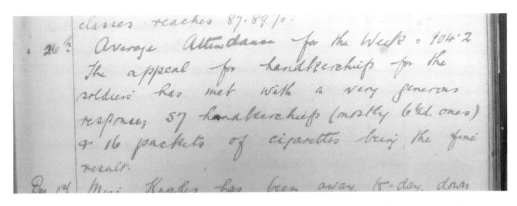

26 November 1915 The appeal for handkerchiefs for the soldiers has met with a very generous response: 57 handkerchiefs (mostly 6½d ones) & 16 packets of cigarettes being the final result.

14 December 1915 Today I am sending off 10/- to the Overseas Club for Xmas boxes for our sailors and soldiers, plus 1/- to the fund for disabled men; both these sums being raised by the children during the past fortnight.

15 December 1915 Three letters have been received by the children from our soldiers thanking them for their presents.

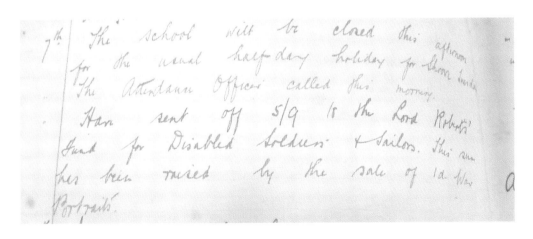

7 March 1916 Have sent off 5/9 to the Lord Roberts Fund for Disabled Soldiers & Sailors. This sum has been raised by the sale of 1d war portraits.

10 May 1916 Mr Reeman[3], an ex-student teacher of the school, now on active service and home from the front on leave, visited us this morning.

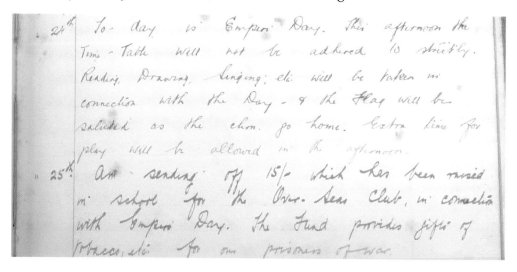

24 May 1916 Today is Empire Day.[4] This afternoon the timetable will not be adhered to strictly. Reading, drawing, singing etc will be taken in connection with the day—and the flag will be saluted as the children go home. Extra time for play will be allowed in the afternoon.

25 May 1916 Am sending off 15/- which has been raised in school for the Over-Seas Club, in connection with Empire Day. The Fund provides gifts of tobacco etc for our prisoners of war.

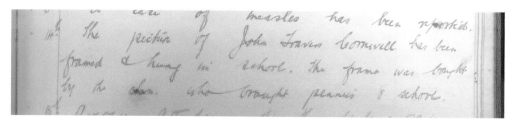

15 September 1916 The picture of John Travers Cornwell[5] has been framed and hung in the school. The frame was bought by the children who brought pennies to school.

3   Mr Reeman was the son of Cllr. Reeman
4   Empire Day reminded children they were part of the British Empire
5   John Travers Cornwell died at the Battle of Jutland and at 16 was one of the youngest recipients of the VC

26 September 1916 Have just sent off a P.O. for 9/6 towards the "Jack Cornwell" Ward, which has been raised by the sale of J. Cornwell stamps.

20 October 1916 Mr L. Reeman called to see us this morning.

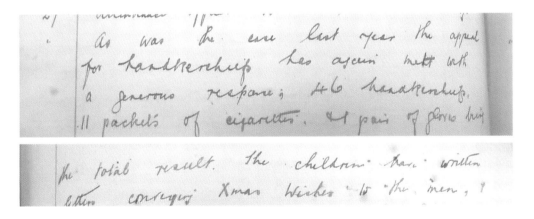

15 November 1916 Mrs G. Ingham and Mrs C. Young called this morning with a request that the children should be asked to bring handkerchiefs again for Middlestown and Overton soldiers' Christmas parcels.

27 November 1916 As was the case last year, the appeal for handkerchiefs has again met with a generous response: 46 hankerchiefs, 11 packets of cigarettes & 1 pair of gloves being the total result. The children have written letters conveying Xmas wishes to the men and these have been attached to the gifts.

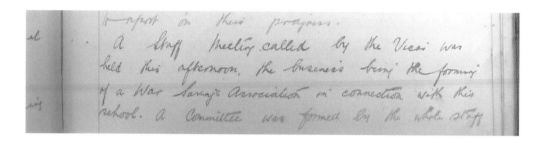

1 December 1916 The Attendance Officer called to see if the recent Air-raid[6] had made any difference in attendance here. If so, the day's marks had to be cancelled. It had not, so the marks were left as usual.

4 December 1916 A staff meeting called by the Vicar[7] was held this afternoon, the business being the forming of a War Savings Committee[8] in connection with this school. A committee was formed by the whole staff and Mr Hudson, assistant master, was elected Treasurer and Miss Gladys E. Peace, Secretary.

12 December Mr Shackleton, Head of the Mixed Department, was elected Chairman.

23 April 1917 Today is St George's Day and this afternoon we are celebrating it by drawing, colouring etc different flags, singing the National Anthem, saluting the flag etc. In addition to this, an appeal has been made for the 'Wounded Horses' Fund and the sum of 6/6 has been gathered from the children and is being sent to headquarters.

---

6   Air raid 1 December 1916
7   The Vicar
8   War Savings Committee

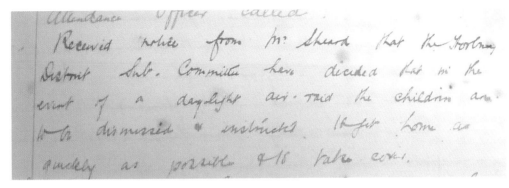

16 January 1918 Received notice from Mr Sheard that the Horbury District Sub-Committee has decided that in the event of a daylight air-raid the children are to be sent home as quickly as possible and to take cover.

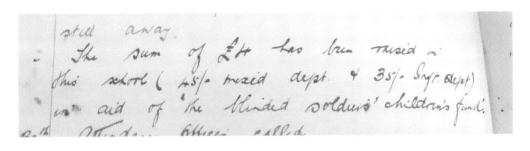

25 January 1918 The sum of £4 has been raised in this school (45/- mixed department + 35/- Infants dept) in aid of the blinded soldiers' children's fund.

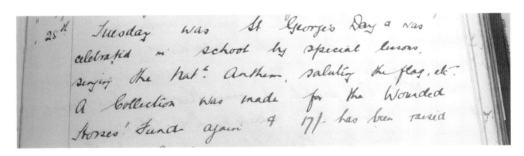

25 April 1918 Tuesday was St George's Day and was celebrated in school by special lessons, singing the National Anthem, saluting the flag etc. A collection was made for the Wounded Horses' Fund again and 17/- has been raised by this Dept.

17 May 1918 Am sending off 10/- collected amongst the children for the soldiers and sailors in celebration of Empire Day.

21 May 1918 The staff is busy now making paper balls which are being sold at 2d each, the proceeds to be given to the Blinded Soldiers' Children's Fund.

14 July 1919 Peace Pageant, Dewsbury

NETHERTON SCHOOL
IN THE
FIRST WORLD WAR

Hilary Haigh

LOG BOOK EXTRACTS

EVENING CLASSES
Gardens at Town End
- Inspected by Frank Reddington, University of Leeds. 10 July 1914.
- Mr Geo Thornton and members of the Education Sub-Committee visited the school this morning and discussed evening school matters generally with the Headmaster. 15 September 1915.

- Mr Coppack B.Sc. (CCI) visited the school this afternoon to consult with the headmaster, on matters pertaining to Evening School work, and particularly regarding the teaching of Horticulture both in Day and Evening Schools. For about half an hour the school was left in charge of Miss Littlewood whilst the Headmaster and Mr Coppack paid a visit to the Evening School's Gardens situated at the Town End.

  Mr Coppack CCI visited the school towards the close of the afternoon session and discussed the closing of the Evening School Garden Plots. 4 December 1916.
- The boys of Standards IV-VII were taken to the evening school garden for the first lesson this afternoon and received a practical demonstration in hoeing between the potato rows of various plots. 18 June 1917.

FARM WORK

- Owing to the scarcity of farm labour, due in some measure to the War, the Education Committee have allowed one boy, Ronald Bentley, to begin work on Messrs Wm. Charlesworth and Sons' Farm, although the boy is only twelve years of age. 15 May 1916.

CURRICULUM

- Lesson on Flowers for 1st and 2nd Infants' classes. 9 July 1914.
- Standards I and II walked to Coxley to examine the 'Branching of Trees' and make observations. 7 October 1914.
- Report of Mr Whaley. 19 November 1915.
- After the close of this afternoon session a lantern entertainment was given to the children by a travelling lecturer. The 'views' exhibited consisted of 'The Chief Buildings of London', unnamed battleships, submarines and illustrations of popular nursery rhymes. 20 January 1916.
- The following stock was received on April 25th:
  - Cambridge Elementary Arithmetics:- St I to VIII inclusive
  - Chambers Effective Readers: 2nd Primer
  - Nelson's Highroads of History: First book
  - Blackie's Stories from Grimm (For St I) 1 May 1916

- Shakespeare Day. At 3 o'clock all the children were assembled in the Central Hall and the Head Teacher spoke to them about the life, works and character of our Great Poet. 3 Shakespeare songs were sung by the elder scholars and old English dances were performed. 3 May 1916.
- Mrs Speight absent…Needlework has not been taken today on account of this absence. Arithmetic has been substituted in all classes. 29 March 1917
- This afternoon the boys of the upper classes were taken into the school garden to plant potatoes, instead of having the usual lesson in handwork.
- Eight boys were engaged in planting potatoes in the school garden this afternoon from 1.30 to 2.30. The rest of the boys were being instructed in Handwork. 2 May 1917.
- The girls of the First Class arranged streamers across the Central Hall before school hours in honour of Empire Day. During the citizenship lessons of the day suitable references were made to Empire Day. Four wounded soldiers from the Wakefield Auxiliary Military Hospital paid a visit to the school during the afternoon and listened to the singing of Patriotic Songs. 24 May 1917.
- Children warned not to use fireworks without a special 'Military Permit'. 5 November 1917.
- This afternoon eighteen children from the Senior Division of the School went to Whitley Farm to pick blackberries - between the hours of 3.30-4.00 under the supervision of Miss E. Earnshaw.
- School closed for blackberry picking at Midgley, Whitley Farm and Hollinghurst. 18 September 1918.
- The children were dismissed at 4pm for a week and a day. The day's holiday was given in commemoration of the effort made by the children in the West Riding towards the National War Savings Campaign. The week's holiday was for the potato harvest. 10 October 1918.
- As a result of the Cessation of hostilities the school closed this afternoon until the morning of 13th inst. 11 November 1918.
- School closed today until 2 December owing to the prevalence of Influenza in the district. 18 November 1918.
- School closed until 9 December, 3 December 1918.
- Owing to the prevalence of Influenza…school closed until 6 January 1919.

- Owing to the prevalence of illness in the village, school closed by MOH. 12 February 1918.
- The Attendance Officer visited the school this afternoon for particulars of the attendance of Edith Ibbotson who has reached the age of fourteen years. Her father objects to allow her to continue at school until the end of term, as required by the new regulations: vide Section 9(1) of the Education Act 1918…In consequence of the action of Mr John Ibbotson in refusing to comply with the section of the Act mentioned, the Education Sub-Committee has decided to take legal proceedings. 9 May 1919.
- At the Wakefield West Riding Police Court on Friday last (May 23rd) Mr John Ibblotson was fined the sum of nine shillings and costs and commanded to send his daughter Edith to school. The girl is present at school this morning. 26 May 1919.
- Mr William Field DCM took up his duties here on the permanent staff as Certified Assistant yesterday the 21st, his studies at the York College being completed. 22 July 1919.
- The school closed at noon today for the Midsummer vacation. An extra week's holiday is given on account of the signing of the "Peace". 1 August 1919.

ARMY

- Mr Brook absent due to medical inspection of applicants to join the 'Sheffield University and Special Battalion'. 10 September 1914.
- Mr Claude Brook leaves school tonight to take up military duties with the City of London Royal Fusiliers. Mr Brook has enlisted for a period of three years or until the end of the War. 30 November 1914.
- Mr Claude Brook visited the school this morning to say goodbye to the teachers and scholars for the present as his regiment departs for Malta on Tuesday next - the 23rd inst. 18 December 1914.
- A rearrangement of the staff has been found necessary owing to the fact that no substitute has been sent to temporarily take Mr Brook's place. Miss Littlewood will take charge of standards III and IV until further assistance can be obtained and Miss Brooke (S) will look after the Infants. 14 January 1915
- Mr Jas Hy Proctor, former assistant at this school, paid a visit. 20 September 1915.

- The Headmaster was absent from school this morning from 10.25 to 11.50 in order in interview the recruiting sergeant and army medical officer at the Horbury Town Hall. Having satisfied these officers as to physical fitness, the Headmaster enlisted in HM Forces under Lord Derby's Grouping System, which enables him to continue his duties at school until 'called up' by the Army Authorities. Permission to enlist had been previously sought and granted by the WRCC per J.W. Horne Esq of the Education Dept. 9 December 1915.
- Private Fred Earnshaw R.E., who, as a scholar attended the St Andrew's Day School in this village, is home for a week's furlough from the Trenches near Loos (France). He expressed a wish to visit this school and see the children at work and as a consequence he spent about half an hour this morning in the various class rooms. He modestly described some of his experiences in actual warfare. 15 December 1915.
- Mrs Speight was absent this morning in order to 'see off' her son, who sails with his regiment to German East Africa on Wednesday. 20 December 1915
- Councillor Reeman's son Mr Lawrence Reeman inter B.Sc (Lond) and Mr C. Brook, formerly of this school, both serving with H.M. Forces, paid a visit here this afternoon and delighted the children with accounts of various places they had visited during the past eighteen months. In December 1914 they set out for Malta where they completed their military training. Later they were sent to Egypt and from there to the Dardanelles where they saw active service. After the evacuation from Gallipoli, in which they took part, they again visited Egypt and last month they were brought to France. 11 May 1916
- The Headmaster was absent this morning in order to submit to a medical examination by the military doctor at Pontefract Barracks, with a view to being accepted by the Army for the period of the War. The examination was incomplete a further visit being necessary. 30 May 1916
- The Headmaster was absent today in order to interview an ear specialist, Dr Whitehead of Leeds. The consultation was made in accordance with instructions received from the Military authorities at Pontefract. 2 June 1916
- Mr Watson went to Leeds University this afternoon with a view to joining the Officers Training Corps
- War bonus is now being paid to Miss Brooke (Supplementary T) at the rate of £3 per annum, the amount being payable from 1st June 1916. The Caretaker

is also to receive an additional war allowance of salary at the rate of £2-11-0 per annum. This allowance will be made payable from 1 July 1916 and will be claimed on this month's salary sheet. The caretaker received a previous 'war bonus' of fourteen shillings per annum, dating from 1 July 1915. The war bonus is paid to other members of staff. 28 August 1916

- The Headmaster received the painful news this morning announcing the death of Mr James Henry Proctor, former assistant master at the school. He was killed in action between 15th and 17th of September. 4 October 1916
- Mr Claude Brook CA of this school, having been invalided home from the war on account of wounds to his legs, paid a visit to the school during the morning session and intimated that he would probably receive his discharge from the army. 9 January 1917.
- Mr Claude Brook having received his discharge from the army resumed duties here today. 18 April 1917
- Miss Effie Littlewood was absent from school this morning from 9.30am in order to see her brother, a member of the Australian Army Corps who is now on his way to France after a brief visit home. 26 April 1917
- Four wounded soldiers from the Wakefield Auxiliary Military Hospital paid a visit to the school during the afternoon and listened to the singing of Patriotic Songs. At noon today nine stones five pounds of nettles which had been gathered overnight by the children, were dispatched to the Military Hospital in Wakefield. 24 May 1917
- Mr Claude Brook CA ceases duty at this school today. On account of his lameness caused by wounds received in the War, he can only reach school from his home with much difficulty; consequently the local Education Sub-Committee have decided to transfer his services to Horbury Council School. 25 May 1917
- School reopened this morning. The Headmaster was absent in order to be present before the Military Medical Board at Wakefield. 4 June 1917.
- Mrs Speight was absent today in order to pay a visit to her son, Corporal George Speight, who is lying ill with wounds at the Glasgow Military Hospital. Corporal Speight has been awarded the Military Medal for bravery in the Field. 17 September 1917 (NB IS this the friend of Fred Earnshaw… cf *Wakefield Express* references)

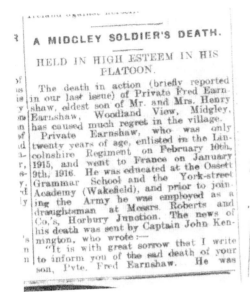

A MIDGLEY SOLDIER'S DEATH.

HELD IN HIGH ESTEEM IN HIS PLATOON.

The death in action (briefly reported in our last issue) of Private Fred Earnshaw, eldest son of Mr. and Mrs. Henry Earnshaw, Woodland View, Midgley, has caused much regret in the village.

Private Earnshaw, who was only twenty years of age, enlisted in the Lincolnshire Regiment on February 10th, 1915, and went to France on January 9th, 1916. He was educated at the Ossett Grammar School and the York-street Academy (Wakefield), and prior to joining the Army he was employed as a draughtsman at Messrs. Roberts and Co.'s, Horbury Junction. The news of his death was sent by Captain John Kennington, who wrote:—

"It is with great sorrow that I write to inform you of the sad death of your son, Pvte. Fred Earnshaw. He was killed in action on the 1st inst. I should have written you before, but the official intimation has only just come to hand. It may be a little consolation to you to know that your son was held in high esteem in his platoon. He was a quiet unassuming boy, who always did his work in a cheerful willing manner. We miss him very much, and our sincerest sympathy is with you and your family in your great trouble."

The last information received by the parents from the deceased was on June 20th, and letters from his friends, Pvtes. Dyson Lowrie and Geo. Speight, both of Wakefield, who stated the last they saw of him was when he was leaping over the parapet; he was waving his rifle to them and was quite cheerful. Pvtes. Lowrie and Speight both worked at the same office with him.

- A special holiday has been granted by the West Riding Education Committee and is taken today in honour of the recent achievement of the West Riding Division in the Battle near Graincourt, France. The children and teachers assembled at 9am and the school was formally opened. In accordance with suggestions received from the WR Education Department, the Special Order of the Day, issued by Major General Walter Braithwaite CB.,DSO., Commanding the 62nd (WR) Division was read. The Headmaster referred to the gallantry and devotion with which the West Riding Men are acquitting themselves in His Majesty's Forces. Special reference was made to the members of the WR forces who have gone from this village and particularly to the teachers and scholars who have been attached to this school. The list includes Mr J.H. Proctor (1911-1912)-killed in action 16th Sept. 1916; Mr Claude Brook (1913-1917)-discharged on account of wounds and Mr Thos. Watson (1915-1917)-at present in hospital- and the following 'old boys'- Angus Hardcastle, Harry Senior, Ben Riley and Wilfred Bowers. A few patriotic songs were sung and the children dismissed. 11 January 1918
- The Headmaster attended Pontefract for the purpose of a medical examination under the National Service Act of 1918 and was put in Grade I: he is therefore likely to be called upon to take up military duties at an early date. 27 May 1918

- The headmaster received instructions to report for military duties at Pontefract Barracks on Saturday June 8th. 3 June 1918
- Mr Claude Brook former Certificated assistant teacher at this school has been appointed temporary Headmaster during the absence of Mr Frank Binns on military duties. 14 June 1918
- Mr William Field of Middlestown, late of the Royal Highlanders, commenced work this morning as Temporary Uncertified Assistan
- Mr Field's salary will be £2-17s per week for each complete week of actual teaching. 8 April 1919
- Having received my discharge from the army in order to resume civil duties, I, Frank Binns take over the charge of this school from today. Mr Claude Brooke will return to Horbury Council School immediately after the holiday. 17 April 1919
- Mr Field has returned to St John's College York to complete his training. 28 April 1919.

AIR RAIDS

- The children were asked to inform their parents that should an air raid occur whilst the children were at school, they would be immediately sent home. 17 January 1917.

PRAYER

- A Prayer for schools in this time of war, authorised for use in West Riding Elementary Schools was received from County Hall. 5 October 1914.

BELGIAN REFUGEES

- Concert in aid of Belgian refugees given in the school hall by children of the school and the Men's Singing Class from the Evening Schools. 30 October 1914.

ILLNESS

- [Middlestown Infants School closed for whooping cough. 2 December 1914.]
- The school nurse visited the school this afternoon and examined a few children suffering from sores on the face. 9 December 1914

- 23 children have been absent from school during the whole of this week. whooping cough and influenza appear to be the causes. The average attendance for this week is only 154, whereas the average for past 12 weeks is 172. 18 December 1914
- The epidemic of whooping cough, influenza and scarlet fever show no signs of abatement and the attendance has fallen below last week's figures. 5 February 1915
- Mr Sheard paid an official visit to the school this afternoon and after examining the numbers present closed the school on account of an epidemic of whooping cough and measles. There are 200 names on roll but of these 62 were absent this afternoon. The percentage present was, therefore, 69%. The schools are to reopen on June 7th. 18 May 1915
- Schools closed another week. 7 June 1915
- …Further week's closure…14 June 1915
-    The school reopened this morning - 140 children being present. Amongst the younger children there is still much sickness…one child - Cyril Kitchen died during the early morning from a chill following measles. 21 June 1915
- Mr Jas. A. Donaldson LDS and a nurse, visited the school this morning and examined the teeth of all children aged 6 or 7. 24 June 1915
- The second death of a scholar - Daisy Brooke - occurred on Saturday. Pneumonia succeeded measles. 28 June 1915
- Mrs Speight is absent today, suffering from influenza. Mrs Speight's absence necessitates to combining of all the infant classes under the charge of Miss Brooke…30 August 1915
- 30 cases of chickenpox. 8 December 1916
- Epidemic illness spreading…upwards of 40 cases notified. 15 December 1916
- MOH instructions for the school to be closed until the expiration of the Xmas vacation – 8 January 1917. 16 December 1916
- School reopened 8 January 1917…premises disinfected during the vacation. Still some cases of chickenpox in the village. 8 January 1917
- Dr Anderson, School MO examined children suffering from adenoids, enlarged tonsils, deafness etc. School Nurse in attendance
- School ordered to be closed…absences due to measles, ringworm and whooping cough. 7 January 1918

- Measles 25 February 1918
- School closed due to outbreak of measles and German Measles. 26 February 1918
- Five children have been taken to Horbury Isolation Hospital, as they are suffering from diphtheria. 27 May 1918
- School closed owing to the prevalence of Spanish Influenza in the village. 5 July 1918
- At noon today, Hilda Labourn, a child in the Babies' class, was knocked down near the Sportsman's Inn, by a motor car, on her way home from school. Fortunately her injuries, though serious, are such as to warrant the medical adviser to expect a recovery. 26 September 1919
- "Armistice Day". In accordance with the expressed wish of His Majesty the King, a total cessation of work was observed from 11am until 11.04am. The children were assembled in the Central Hall at 10.45am. The King's message was read and explained. The horrors of war and the joys of Peace were referred to and attention given to the thoughts of those who by sacrificing their lives had made the present peace possible. At the stroke of 11 o'clock, all heads were bowed in honour of the glorious dead, and two minutes were given up to silent meditation. 11 November 1919.

WEATHER
- There has been a very heavy fall of snow during last night and this early morning: the resulting snowdrifts have made some of the lanes along which the children walk to school almost impassable. The attendance has suffered in consequence and the Babies' Register has not been marked since only two came to school. 19 March 1915.
- As the thermometers in school showed a temperature of only 46 degrees, instructions were given by the headmaster to the caretaker to light the fires today instead of waiting until Friday Oct: -1st – the official date for heating the rooms. 27 September 1915.
- Owing to a heavy fall of snow which has made most of the lanes almost impassable, none of the children under five years of age presented themselves at school this morning, consequently the session was looked upon as a holiday so far as they were concerned and the Babies' Register was not marked. Of the 58 infants upwards of five years only twenty-eight were present.

- A very heavy fall of snow has caused the attendance to fall very considerably today-whereas the number present on Wednesday was 178 - today only 120 are in attendance. 25 February 1916.
- A very heavy snowstorm has made the roads impassable. Only 44 children arrived at school in the morning. A few of those who had come a great distance were delayed - others being wet through were sent home. The registers were not marked. 2 April 1917.
- Very heavy hailstorms prevailed this morning: three children had to be sent home as their clothing was wet through: only 137 children present, 199 on roll. 4 December 1919.

ATTENDANCE

- The number of children on the registers this week reached 196. 23 April 1915
- The attendance officer visited the school this morning to make enquiries concerning four boys who were yesterday working on the Bullcliffe Farm whilst still of school age. 27 April 1915
- Acting upon the instructions of Councillor J. Harrop Esq. CC, Chairman of the local education Sub-Committee, Six boys have been allowed to assist the farmer of Bullcliffe Farm to gather in his potatoes during this week. 25 October 1915.

SCHOOL WAR MEMORIAL

- A School War Memorial has been temporarily fixed on the East wall of the Central Hall. A brass plate 22½ inches by 13½ inches has been mounted on a solid oak (English) frame 38 inches long by 24½ inches wide. The whole has been executed and designed by Mr R. Cecil Hoyle of Dewsbury, from suggestions made by the Headmaster, Mr Frank G. Binns. The cost has been defrayed almost entirely by the teachers and past and present scholars (£18-10-0). 13 September 1922
- At 7.30pm last evening - 13 Sept - the School War Memorial and Roll of Honour was unveiled by Lieutenant-Colonel Pickering DSO, MP of Netherton Hall, in the presence of a crowded audience of parents, old scholars, present scholars and teachers - past and present

The following programme arranged by the Headmaster was gone through:-

1. The Welcoming of All by Mr F.G Binns and
2. Introduction of Chairman.
3. The Chairman's Remarks…Coun Hy Reeman-local representative on the Education Sub-Committee.
4. Hymn "Lest We Forget" (Kipling).
5. The unveiling of Memorial Tablet by Lt. Col. Pickering DSO, MP.
6. Dedicatory Prayer by The Rev: A. E. Hey, Priest in charge of Netherton.
7. Sounding of "The Last Post" by Mr George Speight MM, son of Mrs Speight a member of school staff.
8. The placing of Children's wreaths and flowers.
9. Hymn "O God Our Help in Ages Past".
10. Vote of thanks to Lt. Col. Pickering and others - by Mr Hector Whittell and Miss Nellie Reeman, both old scholars.
11. Hymn God Bless Our Native Land.
12. God Save the King.

Mrs Proctor (mother) and Mr Proctor (brother) of the late James Henry Proctor and Mr and Mrs Walter Bowers, parents of the late Wilfred Bowers, were present.

The inscription on the tablet is as follows:-

To the Memory of
James Henry Proctor (Assistant master)
Wilfred Bowers (an old boy)
Who were connected with this school and
Gave their lives in the Great War
Roll of Honour
Of all those who served
Teachers
Frank G. Binns; Claude Brook; Cyril Dickenson;
Wm. Field DCM and Thomas Watson
Old Boys
Clifford Armitage; Reginald A. Bird; Wm. Bowers;
Willie Hampshire; Angus B. Hardcastle; Wm. Benjamin Riley;
Harry Senior.

It is intended to permanently fix the memorial so soon as the necessary permission is granted by Mr W. H. Brown, on behalf of the West Riding County Council.

- A communication received from the Divisional Clerk (Mr Benj. Sheard) this morning states that the official approval of the West Riding Committee to fix the War Memorial to the school wall is sanctioned. 6 October 1922.

NETHERTON COUNCIL SCHOOL

UNVEILING OF THE WAR MEMORIAL AND ROLL OF HONOUR

For some time the question of placing a lasting memorial in the school to the teachers and former scholar who paid the Great sacrifice during the late war, had occupied the minds of the Headmaster and staff.

An appeal was made by the Headmaster to the old Boys and Girls of the school and the response given was splendid, showing that although school days were past, love for the place where happy days had been spent still lives. The elder scholars still at school asked to be allowed to share in the scheme, and so voluntarily swelled the funds.

It speaks well for the excellent spirit that exists between past and present teachers and scholars, that no outside assistance has been called upon to raise the considerable sum necessary.

A splendid memorial designed and executed by Mr R. Cecil Hoyle of Dewsbury has been obtained and temporarily placed in a prominent position in the school.

On Wednesday evening the Central Hall of the School was packed with parents and past and present teachers and scholars on the occasion of the unveiling ceremony.

At the outset, the Headmaster, Mr F. G. Binns, expressed his pleasure at meeting so many parents, and particularly old scholars and then formally invited Councillor Henry Reeman, as local representative of the school on the Education sub-committee-and as a military gentleman of former days, to take the chair.

Mr Reeman felt it appropriate to be asked to occupy such a position on such a memorable occasion. His connection with the school has extended for most of the time it has been in existence and his interest in its welfare had increased rather than diminished. He reminded all present of the reason of their gathering together and congratulated the teachers and scholars past and present on their generosity. He went on to remind the children of the causes of war and the demands it makes on the young life of the country and the bravery of those who went out to fight from this school - old scholars who suffered privations and loss of life in defending our homeland from the German oppressor and of the many who still suffer as a result of their service.

Continuing, he asked the children to endeavour to live up to the standard of those who had set them such a noble example and to remember for what the memorial stood which Lt Col Pickering DSO was about to unveil. If this be kept in mind, whenever our country should need the service of its sons, Netherton boys brought up in this school should never shirk their duty. Nevertheless, he sincerely hoped there would be no more war.

At this stage, the children and all present sang Kipling's Recessional "Lest We Forget".

Lt Col Pickering, before actually unveiling the memorial spoke of the honour he felt when he had been called upon to take part in the proceedings. He also felt that schools and places of worship were the places where memorials should be placed, for in such places they would teach lessons of great purpose.

This memorial would honour the parents of the soldiers and descendants of their families who would always be able to point to the fact that one of their members strove to do his duty.

Addressing the children he hoped there would be no fighting in their time, but if it were forced upon them again, he urged the boys who would then be young men of the day, to respond to the call and do their duty by defending the old country and its freedom. Some say that if there was another war, the boys would not be so ready to go, but he knew better and he felt sure that then as now Englishmen would do their duty and under similar circumstances prove worthy of the land of their birth by following the example of those whom we had met to honour this evening.

He now unveiled the memorial. Dedication prayers were offered up by Rev. A. E. Hey, priest in charge of Netherton. Immediately followed the "Last Post" by Mr George Speight MM of Wakefield.

Wreaths and flowers were next placed at the foot of the memorial by the relatives of the late J. H. Proctor and Wilfred Bowers who paid the great sacrifice- by Norman Oldroyd (scholar) on behalf of present teachers and scholars and Ruby Wilkinson (scholar) on behalf of the girls of the upper school and Phyllis Blackburn (scholar).

The children next sang "O God Our Help in Ages Past". Following this Mr Hector Whittell (an old boy) and Miss Nellie Reeman (an old scholar) proposed and seconded votes of thanks to Col Pickering for his services this evening to their old school of which they were proud and for the interest which they hoped he would continue to have in the school.

Col Pickering replied, again expressing his appreciation of the honour of being allowed to unveil the memorial and said that he would be only too delighted at any time to do all he could for the N. C. School.

Mr C. Dickinson, headmaster of Woodlesford Council School and formerly assistant master at Netherton in proposing thanks to others who had taken part expressed his thanks for the honour of being invited.

He fully endorsed the Colonel's remarks about the future and looked back with pleasure at the happy time spent at this school. He voiced the feelings of all when he said the ceremony had been most impressive and the singing of the children very uplifting and beyond praise.

The Rev A. E. Hey responded and advised the children to keep in mind the anniversaries of the deaths of the 2, by bringing fresh flowers on those days. The finest and most efficiently organised memorial ceremony concluded with the singing of the hymn God Bless Our Native Land and God Save the King.

Netherton School Log Book, WYAS, Wakefield WMD4/2/34/3

THE WESTERN FRONT

LETTERS
HOME

Sergeant Harry Moxon
2nd Battalion
Yorkshire Regiment
3/6013

9/1904 Richmond Barracks

Address: Pte H Moxon, Reg No 6013, A Company, PWO Yorks.Regt., 3rd Battalion, The Barracks, Richmond, Yorks.

Dear Sister

Just a few lines to let you know how I am getting on. I am now at Richmond Barracks. I set off from Pontefract at 10 minutes past 3 yesterday, and got to York at 4 o'clock. I had to wait there one hour, so I had a look round. I saw the old walls and York Minster. I also had to change at Darlington and wait there 1½ hours, it was about 10 o'clock when I got here. I don't think Richmond is a very big place. The Barracks are up on a hill, they can see a long way out of the windows. It is the Alexandra Princess of Wales's Own Yorkshire Regiment, known as the Green Howards that I am in. I think I shall be up about 7 weeks. Love to all from your loving Brother, Harry

Am now in uniform have got my kit bayonet etc today.

————

10/1904 Richmond Barracks

Dear Sister

Just a few lines to let you know I am getting on alright. We have been having a sham fight today, it was better than drilling. I went to a supper at the Wesleyan Soldiers Home down in the town on Saturday night; there are all kinds of games and books there. There is a Recreation Room and a Reading Room at the Barracks. I generally go to the Gymnasium at night, when I do not go out. We are going to start route marching on Friday. That is once or twice a week they march about 6 or 8 miles away from Barracks and back. I have to clean my belt rifle and bayonet every day and all the other straps once a week. We can go out after 3 o'clock and we have to be back at 9.45 unless we get a pass then we can stop out till 12 o'clock. I am very comfortable in the barrack room. There are 2 fires in and we have five thick blankets and two sheets each. Being in the army is a lot better than I thought it would be. I would not care if I was going to do three years. I know nearly all the rifle exercises now. I am three squads higher than some lads that listed when I did. They all have to be vaccinated when they list, mine are better now. There is a good Band here it goes in front at Church parade. I think this is all I have to say at present. I hope you are all well at home.

From your loving Brother, Harry

Remember me to Joe and Willie Earnshaw and G Gilbey if you see them. The badges are one cap badge and two collar badges.

Note: Harry must have included three badges with this letter. Their present whereabouts are unknown.

————

26.7.1914 Barnard Castle

Just a line to let you know I am getting on alright. How are you getting on with the hay. I suppose it will have been queer weather for it lately as we have had a lot of rain here; it has been cold too. Is the corn looking anything like harvest yet. It is a nice place here for scenery and there is a large Museum here. I knew there was one but had no idea it was the large fine building that it is. Hoping you are all first rate.

————

1.8.1914 Barnard Castle

It is the first time for me to come home next Saturday but if the war cloud does not blow over, I expect I shall get sent somewhere on the East coast instead. They have stopped all leave and will not let anyone go away even for a day. Russia has mobilised; Germany and France are doing the same, then they will mobilise in this country. I should not mind being a few months on the French frontier, which is where they would most probably send the British troops but perhaps it will all be settled by Saturday. As far as I know the binder is alright for starting except that the driving wheel is one cog higher at one side than the other but I think it will work alright.

————

4.8.1914 Richmond Barracks

I was pleased to receive your letter on Sunday, but was sorry to hear that Father is not well, I hope he will soon be better. It will be rather awkward at home if I am not able to come for harvest. The Germans might have waited another month. We were having holiday and sports on Monday but about the middle of the afternoon the bugle sounded the assembly and we had to start pulling the tents down and pack up and march 16 miles over the hills to Richmond Barracks. I think they are waiting for orders from headquarters. Perhaps we shall stay here a bit. I don't want you to be the least bothered about me - as I am quite alright as long as things are alright at home.

————

17.8.1914 Redcar

I was pleased to receive the letters from you and Polly, tell Father to do as he thinks best with the sheep, I expect the bullock of mine would be best kept a bit if there is plenty for it to eat. I expect the war will last for several months at least as it has not properly started yet - it may last a year or two. We are not allowed to leave this place, no one is allowed to come inside without a pass and there are sentries all around with loaded rifles. What shipping there is keeps close to the coast and there are destroyers further out patrolling up and down. I was on guard over the searchlights last night with 10 men.

———

8.9.1914 Redcar

We have been ordered to be ready to go to the front anytime but I do not suppose we shall go just yet as it would not do to send too many troops out of this country till they have got rid of the German Fleet. I expect we shall be here a good bit yet. They have put a lot of extra searchlights along the coast lately and flash them over the sea at night. You need not bother about me as I am alright and I think I can look after myself. I should like to go on the continent for a month or two to have a look around.

———

16.9.1914 Redcar

I was pleased to receive the letters from you and Hubert. Tell Hubert I will bring him a present when I come home. How is young Freddie at Bretton and Edwin at Midgley getting on, I expect Hubert still comes at dinner time. Did you get many rabbits this harvest. We were in tents and as we have only one blanket it was not very warm at nights. We are now in corrugated iron huts. The British and French seem to be doing very well just now. I think they allowed the Germans to get well into France and Belgium so that we could get among them and cut them off. I expect it will be better fighting country and then the Germans will have a lot of forts on their boundary. It will be a bad job for the German people as a terrible lot of their soldiers will be killed compared with ours and I expect they have homes like us. The Germans fight in close formation, that is large masses of men together so that they will have more confidence and when they do win a battle it is by sheer weight of numbers. They cannot get their men to fight like ours in extended order. Our men fight in single lines 3 to paces between each man and so they take more killing than the Germans and then our men are a lot better shots than theirs. The Germans would be nowhere if it was not for their artillery they seem to have some good guns.

22.10.1914 West Hartlepool

I am in charge of the Dock guard today. It is alright. I stop in the Harbour Master's office and every now and then have a walk round the sentries to see if everything is alright. I have some sentries on the dock gates and some in charge of the torpedo nets that stretch across the mouth of the harbour. How are you getting on with the potatoes, I just wish I could come home for a week or so to help to get them up.

11.11.1914 West Hartlepool

I think we shall be leaving here tonight. We have been ready waiting all day for the order to move off. The trains have been waiting at the station since last night. They do not tell us where we are going but I expect it will be Southampton or somewhere down there ready for going across to the continent. We are ready for the front, we take nothing with us only what we can carry in our pack on our back.

13.11.1914 Basingstoke

850 of us left West Hartlepool this morning at 11.00 am. I will write when we get to our destination. We cannot get to know where we are going but I thought I would write so you would know I had moved. I will post this at the next station we stop at.

13.11.1914 Southampton

(10:00 p.m.) Arrived Southampton docks, going on board ship.

————————

15.11.1914 Havre, France

We arrived here after 24 hours in the Channel. We are waiting instructions where to go. We cannot put what we like in the letters or I could write a good long one.

————————

19.11.1914 Havre

We have been at two different camps since we came here. Our regiment has been split into several lots and sent to different places. It is up to the boot tops in mud nearly everywhere. All the tents I have been in have been in fallow fields. I don't think I have seen a grass field since I came here. Milk cattle are tethered in rows in the fields eating rape and mustard. It does not take long to get the people to know what we want. I got all the main words off on the first day or two.

————————

27.11.1914 Rouen

We have had a couple of inches of snow but it has been nice the last two days.

————————

29.11.1914 France

6013 Sgt H Moxon, No.Corp 2nd Yorkshire Regt,
Base Camp, 7th Division, France

Dear Sister
Just a line hoping to find you all well. I am getting on alright, how are things going on at Bretton? I expect mostly same as usual. It is nice country round here something like it is round Bretton only the houses are a bit more fancy. I have written 3 or 4 letters home, ask Bertha when she comes if they got them alright. Hoping you and Tom and young Freddie are in good health. I am first class.
From your loving brother, Harry

———

3.12.1914 Rouen

I am alright, nothing to grumble about and plenty to eat. I have been to three different camps since I came here, most of our Regiment went straight into the firing line as soon as we landed. I happened to be in the Company that was kept back at base. I expect we shall join the others before long.

———

14.12.1914 Rouen

We have had a lot of rain lately, and have had to dig channels around the tents to drain the water away. Rainy weather is not the best sort under canvas - we are camped in a mangold and cabbage field. Most of the French troops wear red trousers and caps and blue overcoats - they do not wear khaki like us. The Germans wear a kind of silvery grey clothes. Do not worry about me being cold or anything else. I have been able to keep warm and dry until now and I get plenty to eat.

———

29.12.1914 Rouen

On Christmas Day we got a present from Princess Mary - a box of chocolates and a card. We had nothing special here this Christmas expect the present we got. I was on outpost duty. I could just do a dinner of roast beef and Yorkshire pudding for a change. The meat is stewed here but we cannot expect to have things as we would like them.

———

1.1.1915 Rouen

I am moving up to the front either today or tomorrow.

————

20.1.1915 The Front

I am up in the firing line, we are stopping in a barn. We are going into the advanced trenches tomorrow night.

————

31.1.1915 The Front

It was snowing last night. The trenches we are in are about the width of the field in front of our house from the German trenches. We can hear them singing the German National Anthem and giving three cheers for the Emperor. Our artillery started shelling them at 6 o'clock in the morning, the shells were just clearing our heads and fairly raining on the German lines. The Germans shell us occasionally but it has been mostly rifle fire up to the present. Just behind my trench is a farmhouse blown down, stacks of unthreshed corn knocked over and cattle lying dead all around.

————

8.2.1915 The Front

I was pleased to receive your letter with the handkerchiefs and buttons - they were just the things I was wanting. I can get plenty of clothes but the things I would like are a bit of cake and a few mints. Just for a change as it is nearly all hard biscuit and tinned beef here. We do (*illegible*) days in the trenches (*illegible*) days out. When we are out of the trenches we are in reserve just behind in empty houses or farms. We are in a state I can tell you when we come out of the trenches - daubed up to the neck in mud. There is no sleep in the trenches as if we happen to keep still too long our feet are like lumps of ice. It is always wet underfoot where we are and we have to keep bailing the water out. The Germans are firing at us and us at them, both with artillery and rifle, day and night. The firing was very heavy last night and the night before. It was a sight to see, the shells bursting in the air half a dozen together and the big guns flashing; it was one big roll like thunder for two hours. They are Bavarians in the enemy's trenches opposite us -

they have some good singers among them and often sing and play mouth organs. We get about two tablespoonful of rum each morning we are in the trenches. I have seen in some of the papers where someone was wanting the Government to do away with the rum ration. But anyone who has had a few nights in the trenches hope it will not be as by morning everyone is nearly dead with the cold and the rum warms one up and gets the blood circulating again. I could fill pages but perhaps I might be saying too much as it all has to be before the censor. We have to dodge out of the trenches at night for water and sticks to make a fire to make tea. It tastes queer as it is always smoked and with no milk. One of the men in my section got killed a couple of nights ago as he was stepping down into the trench with a bundle of wood. We have lost a few men lately.

————

23.2.1915 The Front

I was just passing the church when two shells went through the roof and I went inside to have a look. The shells had made a mess of it inside, a lot of monuments were smashed and most of the woodwork by the alter in splinters. The churches round here are not much to look at outside but they are grand places inside. I think it is a shame the Germans shell them like they do. It is a bit better in the trenches now we have got some pumps and we are putting down boards to stand on. It has been a white frost the last few mornings and it was snowing one night last week when we were in the trenches. Some of the airmen are very daring. I think they deserve a special medal if anyone does. There was one aeroplane up yesterday over the German lines, the German shells were bursting all round him and they were firing at him with machine guns but he did not seem to mind and kept hovering round trying to locate their guns. I have plenty of clothes but there is only one thing that bothers me and that is cold feet with the ground being so wet. A large number of men have been sent to hospital with frost bitten feet. Enclosed is a couple of shrapnel shells burst in the air and scatter the bullets all around.

―――――

2.3.1915 The Front

I thank you at home for the parcel which I received. I could not write until now as we have been in the trenches. We lost a few men this time mostly from shell fire. I am first class, hoping you are all well at home.

―――――

5.3.1915 The Front

We are moving to another position. The Canadians are taking our place.

―――――

9.3.1915 The Front

I write this on the eve of a battle. I am going to put it inside an envelope directed to you with instructions to post it if I get killed. If I am killed in action, I die with a good heart and am not afraid to meet my Maker. If I do not see any of you at home again I hope to see you all in Heaven where war will be no more and German and Briton will be as one. I send my love to Father and you and all my brothers and sisters and relations and friends. May God comfort you and give you long life and happiness. Do not grieve for me. I die for my King and Country as a solider should doing my duty.

From you ever loving son. Harry.

―――――

2.4.1915 Letter from Lt. G F Hadow, Yorkshire Regiment

Dear Mrs Moxon

I am answering your letter as your son happened to be in my platoon and he happened to have been shot in the trench quite close to me on the morning of the 12th. It was during a counter-attack of the Germans. Your son was behaving himself splendidly and it will probably be very consoling for you to learn that he suffered no pain being shot through the head and instantly killed. Your son was buried alongside the graves of other men of this battalion about a mile to the

A SERVICE "IN MEMORIAM."

On Sunday afternoon at Midgley U.M. Chapel, a service was held in memory of Sergt. Harry Moxon, 3rd Batt. Yorkshire Regiment, who was killed in action on the morning of the 12th March, at Neuve Chapelle. The chapel was well filled. At the outset the "Dead March" (Saul) was played by the organist (Mr. George Earnshaw), the congregation standing. Mr. Wm. Challenger (Elsecar) gave a sympathetic address, based on the words "I have fought the good fight" (II. Tim. v., 6). "O God, our help in ages past," "A few more years shall roll," "What are these arrayed in white," and "For ever with the Lord" were sung. Amongst the congregation were members of the Clayton West Ambulance Association, of which the deceased had been an active member. Much sympathy is felt for Moxon's parents and family. The deceased was very well known and respected.

BRETTON WEST SERGEANT KILLED.

Mr. and Mrs. G. P. Moxon, of Pot House Farm, Bretton, have received news from the War Office that their son, Sergeant Harry Moxon, was killed in action during the severe fighting of the last few weeks. Sergeant Moxon had seen a good deal of fighting, and his letters home gave graphic descriptions of the murderous warfare, and wanton destruction of the German soldiers. The news of his death caused a painful sensation in the village, as he was a popular young man, and was well respected by all who knew him.

Harry Moxon Memorial service 17 April 1915 *Wakefield Express* Exp p11

Sgt Harry Moxon obit *Wakefield Express* 1 April 1915 p5

north of the village of Neuve Chapelle. I'm afraid I have put this all very clumsily. Yours truly

Note: Lieutenant G.F.Hadow is commemorated on the Le Touret memorial along with Harry Moxon.

10.4.1915 Letter from L/Cpl F Wood, Yorkshire Regiment

Dear Sir

I am writing to you in regard to your son's death, the late Sergeant Moxon, who was killed in action at Neuve Chapelle on March 12th, 1915. I must say he died a hero and I can tell you he is a great loss to our Company as he was well respected by all the men and also the Officers. I was next to him when he was killed and he never spoke a word before he died. He was shot in the head by a sniper and the same night we dug a fine grave and buried him. I took 2 Princess Mary's Boxes out of his valise and also his watch and his cap badge so I am forwarding you them. I am very sorry for the delay but I have been waiting for your address and I have just received it. Allow me to say it again. Your son died a hero's death and no man in 'B' Company of the 2nd Yorkshire Regiment was so well respected as the late Sergeant Moxon. I can assure you I have lost a good friend - not only me but a good many more.

I remain, yours truly

Note: The present whereabouts of the Princess Mary's boxes, watch and cap badge are unknown

HATS AND HUTS: THE STORY OF THE YMCA WOMEN'S AUXILIARY IN THE GREAT WAR

Sue McGeever

DURING THE FIRST WORLD War women were called upon to do the work that their menfolk had done before. Many of these occupations have been well documented such as nurses, munitions workers, forestry workers and working in factories. The YMCA Women's Auxiliary is less well known despite their important work.

Within ten days of the declaration of war, the YMCA had established no fewer than 250 recreation centres in the United Kingdom, providing a cup of tea, sandwiches or other refreshments, perhaps some reading materials. Many of these centres were at or near railway stations or other places where large numbers of troops would be passing.

In November 1914, the first YMCA contingent went to France and organised similar centres at Le Havre. Later, they were also in operation at Rouen, Boulogne, Dieppe, Etaples and Calais (the principal army bases), Abbeville, Dunkirk, Abancourt (railway junction), Paris and Marseilles. Eventually there were numerous such centres in each of the places mentioned, and another three hundred along the lines of communication. Vast quantities of refreshments were served out to troops on the move: for example, one centre at a railway siding at Etaples served more than 200,000 cups of cocoa each month.

The Huts closest to the front line were staffed by men but women worked in the huts a few miles behind the lines and also at the ports of arrival where

Window at Swaffham Prior, Cambridgeshire. (Photograph supplied by Adrian Barlow)

the troops stayed until they were sent to the Front. Here the troops were able to change their cash for French francs, cash their postal orders and learn a little of the French language. The YMCA had to apply for permission to sell cigarettes. YMCA note-paper, envelopes and postcards were freely available and the ladies would write the message for men who were too badly injured to be able to write for themselves. Away from the Front the huts tried to make the troops feel as though they were at home.

The staff of the YMCA was largely voluntary; mostly female but with some male staff who were over military age or below the medical requirements for active service. At any time, some 1500 YMCA workers were in France and Flanders alone.

In December 1914 the YMCA Auxiliary Committee for women's work was formed with Princess Helena Victoria of Schleswig-Holstein as its President and the Countess of Bessborough as its Honorary Secretary. The Women's Auxiliary was supported by both Queen Mary and the dowager Queen Alexandra. Initially nearly 40,000 women answered the call to volunteer.

Besides the refreshments counter the men could read the newspapers or books from the library. Billiards, board games, cards and dominoes were all provided. Visiting lecturers spoke to the troops; a Padre was on site to conduct evening prayers and to counsel the men and entertainment took the form of sing-songs round the piano, gramophone records and Lena Ashwell concert parties. Outdoors, there were areas where cricket or football could be played. Jessie Wilson had a garden outside Hut 15 at Harfleur. Everything was made to feel as much like home as it could possibly be. Some of the huts away from the front line had a cinema/ concert room. The troops could buy tobacco, refreshments, toiletries and the beautiful French silk embroidered cards.

This account from March 1915 outlines the experience of Cecil Heywood from Middlestown.

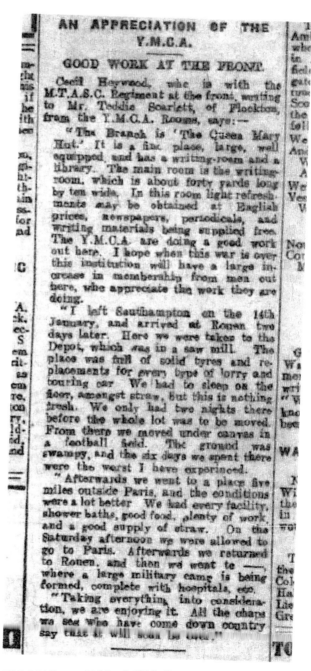

Wakefield Express 13 March 1915 p9

JESSIE MILLAR WILSON.

Jessie Millar Wilson was born in 1871 and was an active campaigner for the Suffragettes. At the outbreak of war Jessie was living in Otley with her sister and brother-in-law.

In 1915, at the age of forty four, she became a YMCA volunteer in northern France working at Hut 15 in Harfleur, close to the port of Havre. She kept a journal of her three years in France which have been edited by Joan Duncan and has been published in the book "Aunt J". This book piqued my interest in the work performed by the YMCA Women's Auxiliary during the First World War.

At Hut 15 in Harfleur, Lena Ashwell gave their first concert on behalf of the YMCA. The concert party arrived on 15 February 1915 and during the next fortnight they gave thirty nine concerts in fifteen days, touring around the 'huts' in Northern France.

Jessie Wilson noted that these concerts were very popular with the troops and the performers included well known music hall artists. War time songs were included for all the troops to sing. Ivor Novello was one of the performers and he wrote "Keep the Home Fires Burning" for this first performance at Havre. It became a great favourite at the concerts. On occasions when there was not any entertainment the hut would organise a competition or tournament. Jessie Wilson explains that prizes, never money, were given and included metal mirrors, letter cases, cigarette holders, pipes and air cushions.

WHAT WAS PROVIDED BY THE YMCA

A great deal of money was required to pay for equipment, staff, subsidised meals, entertainment and items that were provided for the troops such as writing paper, postage, books and soap. Committees set up by local YMCAs raised substantial sums to support this work. Between 1916 and 1918 the Yorkshire Union had flag days, hut weeks and collections which raised £81,553-17s-11d – the equivalent of £4.3 million pounds, today.

BETTY STEVENSON

Betty Stevenson was born in York in September 1896 but the family moved to Harrogate in 1913. Both Betty's parents were active supporters of the YMCA in Harrogate and they were involved with the Belgium refugees who came to the town in 1914.

Wakefield Express 15 January 1916 p3

In January 1916 Betty's aunt went to manage a YMCA canteen in France and Betty joined her aunt at the St Denis Hut on the outskirts of Paris. Betty acquired a car which she initially used to go from the St Denis hut to her billet. As a YMCA driver, she was responsible for transporting lecturers, concert parties and stores.

Throughout her teens Betty had been an avid letter writer and she kept a journal whilst away at school which she sent home to her mother with instructions to 'keep the diaries because I want to copy them into a proper book, when I get home'. She continued to record her life in France.

Betty became a driver for the YMCA for the Motor Transport Scheme based at Etaples, working with relatives of the wounded. In association with the War Office, relatives of dangerously wounded men could travel to France where the YMCA met the boat and they were conveyed to the hospital where the man was lying.

In June 1915, the YMCA opened a hostel in France for the use of relatives visiting dangerously ill men. A YMCA car met the visitors at the port and took them to see their soldier relative. There were in the region of 100-150 such visitors each day. During the whole time the relatives were in France they were entertained as guests of the YMCA in their hostels at the cost of the Association.

Early in March 1918, the German offensive began. Betty with other YMCA personnel volunteered to go each evening to the railway station to feed many fleeing refugees. On 30 May she was killed in one of the many air raids taking place at the time; she was only twenty-one years of age. Betty was posthumously awarded the Croix de Guerre avec Palme by General Petain and she was given a military funeral. In Christ Church, Harrogate there is a memorial to Betty Stevenson YMCA Croix de Guerre avec Palme.

The letters had continued throughout the war years and Betty's mother compiled letters, journals and other correspondence in a tribute to her daughter in 1920.

I have been able to tell this story using contemporary sources.

REFERENCES

Ashwell, Lena (1922). *Modern Troubadours. A Record of Concerts at the Front.* Glyndale publishers.

Duncan, J. E. (ed) (1999). *Aunt* J.: Jessie *Millar Wilson MBE. Wartime Memories of a Lady YMCA Volunteer in France* 1915-1918. W Yorkshire: Smith Settle.

Harrogate Herald. Obituary. 12 June 1918.

Hodder-Williams J.E. *One Young Man. The simple and true story of a clerk who enlisted in 1914.*

Kindle 2011.

Kellett, J. (1920). *That Friend of Mine. A Memoir of Marguerite McArthur.* London: Swarthmore Press.

Red Triangle Bulletins Vols. V & VI (1914-1920, 1919-1929). Held at Birmingham University archives.

Royds Susan. (1919) *A Few Experiences in ... War Zone 1915 – 1919* Birmingham University archives.

Stevenson, C. G. R. and A.G. (1920). *Betty Stevenson YMCA Croix de guerre avec palme.* Longmans. London: Green and Co.: University of California Press. (Available to download for free)

Yapp, K. V. (1919). *The Romance of the Red Triangle.* London: Hodder and Stoughton. (Available to download for free)

YMCA (c1916). *Told in the Huts. The YMCA Gift Book.* London: Jarrold & Sons.

Yorkshire Union of YMCAs - minutes held at Birmingham University archives.

SOURCES OF INFORMATION:

http://www.aberdeenymca.org.uk/worldwar1.htm

http://digital.nls.uk/first-world-war-official-photographs

http://frontforum.westernfrontassociation.com/index

http://www.yretired.co.uk

http://www.1914-1918.net/ymca.htm

http://www.birmingham.ac.uk/index.aspx

WAKEFIELD AND DISTRICT MARINES IN HOLLAND

Hilary Haigh

THE MEN ARE IN GOOD HANDS

Most of the men from the Parish who enlisted were in the army, but some, like Willie Taylor, Willie Lee, James McCall, John Thomas McCall and Tom Townsend were marines in the First Royal Naval Brigade, part of the Royal Naval Division, under the command of the First Sea Lord, Winston Churchill and who had been hastily retrained as infantrymen.

Hardly prepared and barely equipped, their task was to defend, alongside the Belgian army, the Belgian city of Antwerp against the German army and to impede the German progress to France.

By 8 October 1914, however, Antwerp could be defended no longer against the German guns, and the Belgian and German troops were ordered to retreat via the River Schelde.

(The citizens of Antwerp were evacuated, many of them coming to England, among them the de Vos family, who were welcomed to Middlestown).

93

Because the British troops did not receive the order to withdraw in time, they missed the train which was due to evacuate them. Rather than surrendering to the Germans, the British troops, under Commodore Henderson, proceeded over the border, into neutral Holland, where they were interned according to international law for the duration of hostilities.

Over 1500 British troops were accommodated in wooden barracks in Groningen, in what came to be known as the 'English Camp' or 'Timbertown'.

To keep up morale, a daily routine of exercise was established and music, drama crafts and sports clubs set up. The cabaret company 'Timbertown Follies' was very well known. There was rehearsal space within the camp and workshops for the carpenters, furniture makers, tailors and electricians. Furthermore there were classrooms, a small church, a post office and a large recreation room.

Despite the comparative safety of internment, however, there were several attempted escapes in 1915. A few Groningen inhabitants were even imprisoned on account of aiding such attempts.

Later the escapes were stopped because the Dutch and British government came to an agreement. The British received the right to regularly 'go on leave' to the centre of Groningen – sometimes the inhabitants complained of their alcohol

abuse. Even later they received visitation rights allowing them, by word of honour and under certain conditions, to go to England for four weeks (often prolonged to eight weeks).

Also more and more contacts with the people of Groningen were established. A lot of Tommies became regular family friends of families from Groningen and there were courtships and marriages with Dutch girls.

Already at an early stage the interned were asked to become involved in the daily labour process, on a voluntary basis and as much as possible in the area of their original civilian profession. Next to getting out of the rut of military existence, this offered possibilities for more social activities and more pay.

For hiring those interned the Dutch government gave out special permits to prevent them from taking up Dutch jobs. In 1915 the British were put to work at, among others, machine factories and ship building yards in the province of Groningen.

In the city of Groningen the interned had jobs in several small businesses. Next to this during the harvest season many farms, bothered by a dire shortage of staff due to the mobilisation, received help from the British interned.

Firstworldwar.com

The following contemporary reports from the *Wakefield Express* give an indication of the situation in Antwerp from which the Belgians fled, including the de Vos family who came to Middlestown.

This letter from Private Willie Lee to his wife at Middlestown, gives his experiences from the time he left England for the front to arriving at the front:

LOCAL NAVAL BRIGADE MEN AT ANTWERP.

"LIKE A NIGHTMARE."

THE RELIEF GUNS ARRIVED TOO LATE.

During the week six men of the First Naval Brigade, who took part in the defence of Antwerp, arrived in Wakefield for a few days' holiday, and were warmly welcomed at their respective homes.

One of the party was Seaman Oliver Cowling, of Bailey's Buildings, Eastmoor, who was engaged as a cleaner at the Wakefield Post Office. Cowling, an unassuming young fellow, did not care to give a full detailed account of his experiences when seen by one of our representatives. He said that the whole business was more like a nightmare than anything else, and he never wished to go through the same experience again. "When we arrived," he said, "the Belgians had been in the trenches nine weeks and were done up. The Royal Marine Light Infantry had been there about nine days, and then the Naval Brigade were sent out to relieve them. We manned the trenches until a week last Tuesday, and the Belgians retired. The Rt. Hon. Winston Churchill came into the firing-line, and all the men were proud of him. A German aeroplane went up and put smoke rings over the trenches to enable their gunners to find range, and they had two observation balloons. We held on until the refugees and the Belgian army had got out, and then we retired through Antwerp. We could have held out longer but had not sufficient heavy guns to withstand the attack. When we were retiring through Antwerp the relief guns passed us, but they were too late. Buildings were set on fire by the German spies, and we were told that a spy, from a windmill, signalled to the Germans our positions, but we could not get at him. After a tramp of 35 miles we went by rail to Ostend and embarked there. The Germans had a 17" gun firing on the forts, and they fired their shrapnel right over the trenches into the town three miles behind. It was rumoured that one of the German spies was acting as a chauffeur to an officer. He was discovered and shot.

"MIGHT HAVE ONLY BEEN A PARADE."

"MIGHT HAVE ONLY BEEN A PARADE."

Fred Brown, of Charlotte-street, Wakefield, of the Naval Brigade, is another young fellow who is having a few days' holiday after an exciting experience in Antwerp. He appears to be one of those happy-go-lucky young chaps, who treats war as a huge joke. During a conversation with one of our representatives he stated that they were first in Kent, and a week last Sunday they started for "somewhere in France." After crossing the water they started straight for Antwerp, and on reaching their destination the residents gave them a right royal reception, and he believed they would have given their welcome visitors everything they possessed if they had wanted it. "We went into the trenches on Wednesday," he stated with a smile, "and we remained there for three nights and two days. Shells were bursting in all directions, and they came from a wood a considerable distance away. Our men, of course, replied, but I don't know what was the result of our firing. At last the Germans were sending their shells not far from our trenches, and our men continued to reply, the result being that the efforts of the enemy slackened. They had, however, found the range, and when they had quietened down a bit our officers evidently thought it was time that we cleared out. At any rate we received orders to get out of the trenches, and our retirement was quite orderly. There was not the slightest signs of excitement, and we might have only been on parade. We walked through Antwerp, with the German shells far behind." Brown added that while the firing was going on the Rt. Hon. Winston Churchill drove through in a motor-car.

Wakefield Express 17 October 1914

FLEEING FROM ANTWERP.

A GRAPHIC ACCOUNT BY A WAKEFIELD TRADESMAN.

"ONE OF THE MOST PITIFUL SIGHTS ONE COULD IMAGINE."

ENGLAND'S DEBT TO BELGIUM.

A BELGIAN BOY SCOUT SENT TO WAKEFIELD BY MR. GLEDHILL.

Mr. Herbert H. Gledhill, of the Waterproof Stores, Little Westgate, Wakefield, who has also a business at Utrecht, Holland, writing from the latter place on Oct. 12th, to his wife, says:—

"I see you are getting Belgian refugees. There are many thousands in Utrecht. Figures are not obtainable, but at a guess 4,000 or 5,000, and every hour more arriving. I see in the "Wakefield Express" there is a letter, in which the writer says the Local Government Board have given the impression that little or no further help will be necessary. In Holland, however, there are about a million, or getting on that way, and that is very large considering the whole population is only about six millions. In addition there are thousands of Belgian, English, and German soldiers here. 25,000 of these came over the frontier during the last few days. They had been fighting at Antwerp. I saw 5,000 or 6,000 Belgian soldiers myself yesterday passing through Utrecht. Last week I was

on the Belgian-Dutch frontier in the towns of Breda, Rozendaal, and Bergenop Zoom. The train from Breda was full of them. They had just left Antwerp, and they were hoping to get a boat to Flushing. I talked to many of them, and they said the Germans were bombarding the town so heavily that the buildings were being destroyed and that the greater part of the city was on fire. We could see it was ablaze from the train in which we were travelling, the horizon being lit up. In Bergenop Zoom they told me 25,000 fugitives had arrived there the day before, and on the following day I should think 50,000 or 60,000 came in from Antwerp. Most of them were walking, and some in motors, carriages, and vehicles of all kinds. There was a never-ending stream over the frontier all day. I saw churches with all the seating taken out and straw placed along the sides. In one church I saw lying down probably 300 or 400 persons, and when all buildings and houses were full thousands had to remain in the streets with no covering, and only such luggage as they could carry. Bread, milk, and food was unobtainable—there was none. It was one of the most pitiful scenes one could imagine. Thousands of young children without anything to eat, and crying for food which their parents could not give them. This scene was enacted in Breda, Lillry, and Borendaal, and all the towns on the Dutch-Belgian frontier.

Wakefield Express 17 October 1917

On Sunday Oct 4th we received orders to pack our kit and bags, and fall in marching order, preparatory to proceeding to Dover. We arrived at Dover at 3.20pm, where we spent the next twelve hours in loading our transport ship which was to take us to an unknown port in the early part of Monday. We left Dover with an escort of six destroyers and in five hours we found ourselves in Dunkirk harbour, where we disembarked, spending the remainder of theday unloading and transferring to a transport train, which we found was to take us to Antwerp. This being finished we all had a drink of tea, after a day's hard work. The remainder of the evening was spent in providing ourselves with as much ammunition as we could carry. Besides our rifle we had an haversack and leather gear, the latter being filled to its utmost capacity with biscuits and both war and personal belongings; the total weight being over 70lbs. we had to go ahead, as our Allied troops around Antwerp were in a critical position. Afterwards we rode in a third class carriage, which was very narrow and uncomfortable; and at Ghent we discovered that the axle of our carriage, through friction, was heating, and the train had to be stopped. We had then to get into a second-class compartment, in which we managed to get a little sleep.

We arrived at Antwerp about four o'clock on the Tuesday morning, and although so early, we received quite an ovation, in addition to sandwiches, coffee etc, which came in abundance. We marched through the city amidst tremendous cheering. After marching for some considerable time our progress was hindered by drenching showers of rain. However, we found ourselves at a deserted house intended to be our headquarters, but upon receiving an urgent call from the Belgian trenches we immediately set off to their assistance, their position being west of Antwerp. This call necessitated a forced march, as we found it was impossible to reach them as the crow flies, so we set off for about two miles walk, and gradually wheeled round to the south-west of the trenches. After proceeding in the direction for a further three miles, we found we were quite unable to reach them owing to a heavy shrapnel bombardment by the Germans, and to approach the trenches under that heavy fire meant annihilation of practically our whole army, so we returned and made a detour of the city, which brought us to a set of unoccupied trenches two miles outside Wilroch.

Mr Winston Churchill very active

Just as we were making our detour of the trenches we were greeted by the First Lord of the Admiralty (Mr Winston Churchill), who was very active in doing all that he could to bring success to our errand, which was to cover the retreat of the Belgians, thus enabling them to join the French Northern Army, and also to allow the inhabitants of Antwerp and its suburbs to quit in safety. The next three hours we spent in improving our earthworks, and after receiving information from the Belgian scouts to the effect that the Germans from the direction of South East, with very heavy artillery, were in strong force, we were once again compelled to change our position, and at the same time to extend our line, which entailed a long and tedious march. Rain fell in torrents all day, and the roads became exceedingly heavy. At 10.30 the same night we were posted on the outskirts of Nurtrell, when each man got his portion of a meal, and although under fire, those who could settle down to sleep did so.

The Belgian artillery passed us during the same night to join the French army. The sights we saw on this last march were vivid and almost haunting, for although everything spoke of busy life there was an unending stream of Belgian artillery, cavalry and infantry on the one side and the absolute silence of civilian life on the other. The whole thing was one never to be forgotten. Beautiful houses and buildings, commanding good positions, were utilised by the Belgians. Woods etc were also destroyed and converted into death traps and obstruction in an undaunted manner to try and save their country from the bullying, unjust, and undeserved invasion.

Getting it 'Real Hot'

The worst, however, was still to come. Our new position took the shape of a semi-circle, bordered by forts, each fort commanding an opening of about 100 yards, after which came woodland and a few farm buildings. In front of each fort were barbed wire entanglements and spiked footfalls to check the advance of the cavalry. It must be borne in mind that practically the whole of the Belgian armry were well on the way to join the French army. Besides this the majority of the people had been enabled either to take the boat to England or travel by road to Holland, so that as a city Antwerp itself was dead.1 The first move of our Commanders was to perfect the redoubts, also to construct bomb proof shelters and communication trenches. Everything was progressing very satisfactorily. The trenches were practically completed and a meal partly cooked but soon we were startled by the hiss and crash of shrapnel. This was our first intimation that the Germans were near, and, moreover, knew our exact position, but it could hardly be wondered at, when suddenly remembering that a taube aeroplane had passed over our position earlier in the morning, and had luckily escaped the shell from the Belgian guns. All the time shells were being literally shot into Antwerp, and it seemed as if the enemy intended marching up the city and afterwards to turn their attention to us. About an hour after the first shot cam we began to get it real hot. Six guns at least must have been turned upon our company's trenches alone. At all times we could hear the reports of the guns, and then we felt the contents among us.

The Colonel killed

Four shells fell within twenty yards, earth was thrown about, and occasionally men buried in the trenches had to be dug out-circumstances permitting. Things soon became disorganized, as our colonel had been struck with shrapnel, and taken to the hospital in a critical condition. We heard with regret afterwards that he died on his way there. Things went on like this until it grew dark, when the burning oil tanks in the city made the position look gruesome. Men were shivering with cold, and did not seem to recognise one another. Sentries during the night were posted at the trenches, whilst their comrades took what rest they could; in fact all were resigned to meet the enemy before morning. To make things worse the searchlights from the forts nearest to us were put out of action, and we had to strain our eyes and ears in the darkness.

Many Men Lost

It was about 10am when we received information to return to the city, and to take as much ammunition as we could carry. We were told to proceed along the railway line and afterwards we left the railway track for the outskirts of Antwerp. All this time we were under fire from the enemy and eventually we reached a waste bit of ground across which we went in parties of twelve. In spite of those precautions, however, we lost many men, but the rest of the journey was done in safety. We kept on marching for three or four miles further until we came to the docks of the Wilson liners, whose sheds were completely crammed with live stock, whose bellowings and groanings were painful to hear. It was first thought we should here embark for England, but we soon learned different. After a while we boarded a steamer, which took us across the river in a seaward direction, and we disembarked on the Southern Bank-very tired and weary in limb, but not in spirit. We then went up a paved road, which was crowded with carts, bicycles etc, which were being trundled along by poor refugees. Along this road we marched in an orderly fashion for about six miles, until we came to a village, where we were allowed to rest in a field, and although the grass was damp everyone was thankful for the rest. We stayed here for a couple of hours, which only seemed to us as many minutes.

A long tramp towards Ostend

Once more on the road we marched mile after mile along vast stretches of country towards Ostend, the road always being occupied by homeless refugees. About mid-day a halt was made, and a portion of raw meat was given us, and we were all preparing to make ourselves comfortable for a while, when once again we saw a German aeroplane passing over us at a great height. At once orders were given to move on again. Mile after mile went, and we were now becoming exhausted but we managed to tramp along to a railway station called St Gillies. Here we intended taking train for Kulst, the nearest place in Holland, but we were not to be let off so easily. Through some misunderstanding on the railway it was found impossible to take us by rail, so we had to march the remaining four miles into Holland, where we had no other alternative but to hand over our arms and prepare for another night in the open streets, though some of our chaps were fortunate to obtain shelter. The most of us slept on straw on the road, and the night was very cold. Next morning we were early astir,

OVERTON.

NEWS FROM THE FRONT.—A letter received by Mr Walker Allott, of Overton from James McCall, who is a prisoner of war in Kaserne Groningen, Holland, says:—

"I have written to you before, but don't know whether you have got them or not; there are so many letters going through the post that they get lost. I have got sick of being made up in prison I can tell you. We are living very roughly here—a right good feed would do us good; and a good fire, for we have not seen any since we left England; so you can tell how we feel. We have had a very hard time of it since we left home. It would have done you good to have been with us in Antwerp, to hear the cannons roar and the bullets screaming over our heads. It was awful; it was nothing but more murder for us; and such a sight to see the men, women, and children lying in the streets, some with their heads blown off; and others with arms and legs blown off; and some with their insides hanging out. It some with their insides hanging out. It was a shocking sight. I have both gone through something and seen something since I left home. It would have made your flesh creep. Those poor folk who have done nothing wrong. The Germans are nothing but ——: all they come across they murder; they spare none; all have to go under. I was under shell and rifle fire for 60 hours at once, and did not know what minute it might be my turn to fall. My pals on either side of me got shot. It was time then to feel a bit queer, but we had to stick while we got orders to retreat. We got orders to fix bayonets, going through the wood; we were expecting meeting the cold-hearted —— ; but as luck let we didn't, and we were not sorry, for we were all done up. We marched 54 miles in 22 hours, and we were all paid out. I will tell you more when I get back home."

Wakefield Express 5 December 1914 p4

and on our way to Kulst. We arrived there about breakfast-time, where we entrained for Tamusen, and arrived there in the afternoon of Saturday October 10th. We stayed here a while, and then took boat for Flushing. We were then entrained for Trewarden, where we arrived on Sunday, and we stayed here for about a week, and then we got orders to fall in with all our belongings for another destination, Groningen, where we have stayed ever since.

Wakefield Express 2 January 1915

We have received from Mr H. H. Gledhill, Little Westgate, the following interesting letter. Mr Gledhill has a business in Holland, and he is this week paying a short visit to Wakefield. He writes:

The Dutch have made great sacrifices for the Belgian refugees, and Dutch soldiers have gone without food many times in order to give it to them. The mother of my errand boy has taken a child in, and they are very poor. The Belgians who are here, are afraid to go back. If they go, they must run trains to carry German troops and rebuild fortifications for the German Army. This they will not do.

I have been to Groningen and Lieuwarden. In the former place there are 900 Royal Marines, and in the latter place 600. They came over the Dutch frontier when Antwerp fell, in order to prevent themselves being annihilated or captured by the Germans. There are about a dozen of them from Wakefield and district. At the end of this letter I give their names and addresses. I am sending a postcard to their relatives letting them know they are alright and in good hands. They are in military barracks where they must remain until peace is declared. The Dutch are very kind to them. I went with the Rev. H. H. Coryton, Chaplain, English Church, Rotterdam, to look out for recreational rooms for them. In Groningen there are some wooden buildings which were built for an exhibition. Two large rooms will be taken there. In Lieuwarden there is a beautiful building which was specially built for the Dutch soldiers as a recreation room. The Dutch soldiers are all on the frontiers, so the gentleman who gave and endowed the building has offered it to the British Marines. Here they can play games, write, have concerts etc. Tea or coffee costs 2 cents per cup, which is under ½d. There is nothing whatever to pay for the use of the building. They will have fields so they can play football etc. Three churches have been offered so they may have divine services. Hundreds of books have been sent for their use, they may walk in the towns quite free from 5 to 9 in the evenings. Mr Coryton has now very little to do in Rotterdam, as there is so little shipping. The inhabitants of these towns are very friendly towards them, everyone saying "Goodnight" as they pass, they have all learnt so much English. I was allowed into the barracks in order to talk to them, and to find out if there were any from Wakefield. They had had a hot time in Antwerp. During the bombardment I was staying in a small town just on the Belgian-Dutch frontier. At night the doors and windows rattled so much with the vibrations of the firing, one might imagine one was on an express train. The thunder from the guns was terrific. It must have been hell in Antwerp. The British could not hold out against modern siege artillery. The British had taken naval guns with them, but were unable to mount them. The guns in the forts were outranged by those of the enemy. I am glad to say the British guns were got away.

The names of the local men are as follows:-
T. Schofield, 28, Scarborough Street, New Scarboro'
T. Slee, 5, Well Street, Flanshaw Lane, Alverthorpe
Fred Kitchen, Spring End, Horbury
William Gordon, worked at Sykes Athletic Works, Horbury
Wood Frobisher, Warmfield, near Wakefield
Herbert Bolton, 48, King Street, Normanton.
Fred Lands, High Street, Normanton
Fred Newman, 31, Lee Brigg, Normanton
John Thos McCall, Middlestown
James McCall, Overton
Tom Townsend, Middlestown
Wm. H. Lee, Middlestown
English, greengrocer, Normanton
Hughes, 20, Woodhouse Mount, Normanton
Scott, White Swan, Normanton

… I may not have seen them all, in fact I did not as I arrived in Groningen so late, and it was too late to go round the barracks. I had to leave at 7 in the morning by train. I had also got the names of several Leeds and Rotherham men. I am writing to their families to let them know they are safe.

Wakefield Express 31 October 1914

Letters have been received from Private James McCall (Overton) and Privates Thomas Townsend and Willie H. Lee (Middlestown) who are in the Royal Marines, and who were taken prisoners on the crossing of the Dutch frontier after the fall of Antwerp.

Private James McCall, writing from Leewarden, Holland, to his wife, says: "We have been in the firing line. You might have seen in the papers that we were all cut up, but I am pleased to say that we were not. There were a lot of us missing. We walked 54 miles in 22 hours, so you can guess what a time we had…I could tell you more, but we dare not. I think we shall be home soon…you must not be downhearted…Tell all my friends I am safe once more after a very hard time."

Private W.H.Lee, writing to his wife on Oct 20th, says: "I have just received 1s.6d, which is the first money we have had since we left Walmer. We have not had a towel to dry ourselves on, so you can guess it is pretty rough out here. I wish the war was over, as it makes me worse when I don't know how you and my children are getting on. I wrote for the 'Wakefield Express' and 'Sports Echo' to be sent on to me, but I have not received them yet."

Private Lee, writing to his brother, Mr Edward Lee, Middlestown: "We have had it pretty hot up to now…We have had plenty of shipping about to do since we left Walmer, but we have done it, and would have done more if we had been wanted, as it is all in the run of the game. I expect you will have read the papers about us. We have been well cared for where we are now. They are a kind hearted lot of people. They don't know when they have done enough for us…

We cannot get any woodbines around here…We marched about 53 miles in 22 hours, so you can bet we are dead beat. We have not had our boots off for a week, but you see we have to be careful what we put in our letters in case they get into strange hands. You can tell Mother not to be downhearted, as I am not. I have had to go through it, but I am willing to go through it again for my country if it is needed?"

Private Thomas Townsend, writing to his mother from Holland on Oct 13th, states that they are not allowed out of barracks, as they are prisoners. He adds: "We had a very hard time of it when fighting, and I don't care how soon the war is over, as it is very weary here now…

In a letter on Oct 20th he states that they have been removed to Kareme, and he is tired of being a prisoner. He says he feels "very sad and weary", as he has had no letter for four weeks.

Wakefield Express 31 October 1914

INCOMPLETE RECOVERIES: THE MEDICAL EVACUATION OF MIDDLESTOWN AND NETHERTON MEN

Christine E. Hallett
(University of Huddersfield)

THE FIRST WORLD WAR'S Home Front is often associated with the forced jollity of the music hall – a place in which people could forget, or, perhaps, choose to ignore, the realities of war by immersing themselves in the sentimentality of popular songs.[1] Yet, one music hall song lacks the deliberate cheeriness of many others *There's a Long, Long Trail A-Winding* - one of the most frequently-played pieces - whilst never acknowledging the fear and suffering that underlay the real experiences of so many combatants, recognises the fact that not everyone escaped the front lines.[2] It evokes a sense of journeying from an unnamed place to a home that is beautiful, safe and serene – a place where nightingales sing, and the moon beams. Written in 1913 in the USA, when war still seemed only a distant possibility, it was re-published in London in 1914, and became massively popular among British soldiers from the earliest months of the conflict. Its expression of longing rather than expectation, and its evocation of the calm and peace of a home that is more imagined than real, has ensured its survival as a poignant emblem of the war.[3]

---

1   John Mullen, *The Show Must Go On: Popular Song in Britain during the First World War* (London, Routledge, 2015)

2   Zo Elliott and Stoddard King, *There's a Long Long Trail A'Winding*, London Edition (London, M. Witmark and Sons., 1914). Note: Elliott reported that he first wrote the song as a response to the retreat of Napoleon's army from Moscow in the early nineteenth century.

3   The song has been reproduced most recently as part of the BBC television series, *The Crimson Field*, Episode 5 (London, BBC, 2014); and in a new version by British Folk Group, 'Harp and a Monkey': *War Stories* Album (2016)

The song's purpose seems to have been to allay the fears of men who knew that there was no guarantee that they would escape 'active service' with their lives. Indeed, the certainty that some would die without seeing their homes again lent it a power that belies its simplicity. Over 800,000 British men were killed on active service during the First World War. Many died instantly – or within a few hours of being wounded – on the battlefields. Others found their way back from no-man's-land, into the so-called 'lines of evacuation', only to die later 'of wounds'. The majority of British servicemen did make it back home alive, but many would live the remainder of their lives with severe, life-changing injuries or illnesses.[4] As the war progressed, British non-combatants on the Home Front became increasingly aware of the horrors associated with front-line warfare. Even before they were forced to confront the implications of the enormous casualty-lists associated with assaults such as those at The Somme (1916) and Passchendaele (1917), they were learning to associate the war with death and mutilation on a large scale. Perhaps it was, therefore, inevitable that the darker the horror became, the more brightly shone the idea of safe return. In Middlestown, Midgley, Netherton and Overton a cluster of small mining communities in the Eastern foothills of the Pennines – just as in every other part of the British Isles - the fear that loved-ones might not come back home stood as a dark shadow over people's lives. And, as war dragged on and more and more men enlisted, or (from 1916) were conscripted, into the armed forces, the casualty lists grew. Recent research has enabled the re-evaluation of those lists, and has made it possible for the descendants of the men who went to war to remember them in new ways. The recent *A Parish at War* project at Middlestown, Midgley, Netherton and Overton in West Yorkshire has traced the backgrounds of thirty-three, men belonging to the parish of Middlestown with Netherton.[5] Indeed, in some respects, the present community now has more information about what those men experienced than their own neighbours of a century ago. Ironically, we are more aware of the men who did not make it back home – whose journey

4   Christophe Declercq and Helen Baker, 'The Pelabon Munitions works and the Belgian village on the Thames: community and forgetfulness in outer-metropolitan suburbs', *Immigrants and Minorities*, 34: 2, 151-170.

5   *A Parish at War*, Parish Records, St. Luke's Church, Overton, West Yorkshire.

along the "Long, Long Trail" was curtailed by death - than of those who returned to resume their lives after the war. The final resting places of those who died are marked by gravestones erected by the Imperial War Graves Commission, and their short lives are being carefully commemorated by those who attended St Luke's Church long after their deaths.

In reality, the medical evacuation of the war's wounded was a complex and changing process; it evolved quite rapidly during the last five months of 1914, after which it underwent further, more gradual, reform and reshaping. Mark Harrison's *The Medical War* has revealed the unpreparedness of the military medical services in August 1914.[6] Medical evacuation was a slow and cumbersome process. Men wounded during the early battles of the war, at places such as Mons and Le Cateau, were removed from the battle-lines by ambulance workers using horse-drawn carts, their wounds festering under hastily-applied bandages. By the end of September 1914, it was becoming very clear to senior medical officers that men were dying unnecessarily. In an era before anti-bacterial drugs, any delay in the treatment of contaminated wounds heightened the risk of rapidly-spreading infections that could quickly become irreversible. The heavily-manured soils of Flanders and Northern France contained many millions of bacteria of the so-called 'anaerobic' type – microorganisms that thrived in the warm, moist airless environments at the wound-beds of the deep and extensive injuries caused by industrial weapons such as machine guns and shrapnel shells. Veteran surgeons of the Second Anglo-Boer War – accustomed as they were to the management of wounds contracted on the dry, dusty South-African veldt - were becoming painfully aware that the wounds they were seeing now in regimental aid posts and military hospitals had no precedents. They soon recognised that treatment-delay was associated with higher mortality rates. By the end of 1914, they were beginning to get a grip on the logistical problems associated with medical evacuation: motor-ambulances had replaced horse-drawn waggons on most parts of the Western Front; and surgeons were experimenting with a range of treatments for anaerobic infections.[7]

---

6   Harrison, Mark, *The Medical War: British Military Medicine in the First World War*
     (Oxford, Oxford University Press, 2010)

7   Hallett, Christine E., *Containing Trauma: Nursing Work in the First World War*
     (Manchester, Manchester University Press, 2009); Hallett, Veiled Warriors, passim

Among the most significant reforms in military medical evacuation was the insertion of new 'stages' in the lines of evacuation. Instead of trying to remove men from the so-called 'zone of the armies' and bring them back to bases (which could be anywhere between 30 and 100 miles away) before commencing treatment, senior medical officers were experimenting with ways of bringing surgical treatment much closer to the fighting-front. If clinicians could be brought to the wounded, rather than vice-versa, valuable time could be saved. If men could be offered expert treatment for wound shock within just a few hours of their wounding, and stabilised to the point at which they could survive even the most complex surgical treatments, infected material could be cut from within and around their wounds, and antiseptic treatments to eradicate any remaining bacteria could be commenced. Casualty clearing stations (CCSs) became the pivotal points on the evacuation chain – the places at which lives were lost or saved.[8]

As treatment-regimes became more ambitious the need for expert clinicians became more acute. As well as posting medical officers to these small field hospitals, the military medical services took the decision that nurses would also be permitted to serve within them. The proposal that female nurses should serve close to the front lines was welcomed by many of the nurses themselves – including the Matron-in-Chief of the Queen Alexandra's Imperial Military Nursing Service, Ethel Hope Becher, and her deputy on the Western Front, the Matron-in-Chief for the British Expeditionary Force in France and Flanders, Maud McCarthy. Nurses were posted to CCSs from base hospitals, and by the end of 1914, wounded men could be offered expert surgical and nursing care within ten miles of the front line trenches.[9] The lines of evacuation became established and each wounded man followed essentially the same 'long trail' home to Britain – the place that came to be affectionately known as 'Blighty'.

---

8   On the work of clinicians in casualty clearing stations, see: Iain Gordon, *Lifeline. A British Casualty Clearing Station on The Western Front, 1918* (Stroud: The History Press, 2013); Henry Owens, *A Doctor on the Western Front. The Diary of Henry Owens 1914–1918* (Barnsley: Pen & Sword Books Ltd, 2013); Mark Harrison, *The Medical War*; Christine E. Hallett, *Containing Trauma*; Christine E. Hallett, Veiled Warriors, 67-54;

9   Christine E. Hallett, *Veiled Warriors*, 67-54; John Stevens and Caroline Stevens, eds., *Unknown Warriors. The Letters of Kate Luard RRC and BAR, Nursing Sister in France 1914 – 1918* (Stroud: The History Press, 2014).

In the first hours following his wounding, a man's survival would depend on two factors: the extent to which he was capable of applying his own dressing, and the rapidity with which stretcher-bearers were able to reach him and apply more complex emergency treatments such as tourniquets and pressure-dressings, to arrest haemorrhage.[10] During large assaults and at times of heavy enemy shelling there could be a long delay at this first point in the evacuation chain, and many of the most severely wounded men bled slowly to death, while waiting for rescue.

Once removed from no-man's-land, the wounded man – now a 'patient' in the hands of the Royal Army Medical Corps – would be carried to a regimental aid post. Many very severely wounded men managed to drag themselves slowly to their own aid posts – often assisted by 'walking wounded'.

A large proportion of those men who died were lost on the battlefield before they were even able to embark on a journey of recovery. Signaller Wilfred Kaye had been born in Kirkburton on 5 May, 1889. His father, Wilson Morley Kaye was Caretaker to the St Luke's Church and School. Wilfred, a server at the Middlestown Co-operative was a gifted musician. He sang in the church choir and often played the violin as part of a trio with two friends. He died at the Battle of Poelcapelle, one of the later actions of the Third Battle of Ypres, on 9 October 1917.[11] He was just one of the tens of thousands of men who died during the Third Ypres Campaign. At Poelcapelle men already worn out by the assaults of August and September were living in makeshift trenches composed of little more than lines of shell-holes connected by shallow ditches. Because the Allies had already successfully advanced about six miles from their position at the start of the campaign on 31 July, no-man's-land was a vast wasteland of mud, churned-up by a series of heavy artillery bombardments that had disrupted the water-courses and flooded many square miles of territory. Stretcher-bearers had greater difficulty finding and recovering men than ever before, and many of the wounded were lost in what must have seemed to be an endless swamp of mud. Wilfred Kaye's body was never recovered. Yet the anonymity of his death seems to have spurred his family and community into greater efforts than had

---

10   Emily Mayhew, *Wounded*

11   'Wilfred Kaye' *A Parish at War*, Accounts by Hilary Haigh, Parish Records, St. Luke's Church, Overton, West Yorkshire.

been made for men with known graves. As well as being named on the vast Tyne Cot Memorial near the village of Passchendaele (along with over 11,900 of his fellow soldiers), and on his parents' gravestone in Kirkburton Churchyard Wilfred Kaye is remembered by one of most striking memorials of the post-war period: a stained glass window at St Luke's Church, which depicts Saint Wilfrid and which was dedicated to him in 1920.[12]

More is known of the death of Herbert Howden, one of two sons of Elizabeth and Alfred Howden of Middlestown. Herbert had enlisted in 1914, and had been serving the Army in France as a driver with the 71st Brigade of the Royal Field Artillery, when he was wounded at the First Battle of the Scarpe, an assault of the Battle of Arras. It was reported later that Herbert had 'died of wounds', and so it seems highly likely that he was retrieved by stretcher-bearers from the battlefield and taken to a regimental aid post. It is not known whether he survived beyond this point. He is buried in Duisans British Cemetery, Etrun.[13]

Herbert's brother, Bernard, had already been killed at the Battle of the Somme the previous July, and was commemorated on the Thiepval Memorial. Prior to their enlistment, Bernard and Herbert Howden had been living in cramped accommodation – a four-roomed house on Thornhill Road in Middlestown, with their mother, stepfather, three sisters and their stepfather's granddaughter. Bernard had worked in one of the local mines, and Herbert, having spent part of his teenage years as a rope ender in the pit, was employed as a blacksmith. For the Howden brothers, enlistment in the armed forces, and the opportunity to serve overseas must have seemed like an opportunity to escape the grinding monotony of their daily lives. Their deaths were a betrayal of their faith in the political and military system that had drawn them into the war, and their loss, within six months of each other, must have been a shattering blow to their family.[14]

At regimental aid posts, patients' wounds were assessed, and they were given morphine to relieve pain and shock, and anti-tetanus serum to prevent one of

12   *A Parish at War*, Accounts by Hilary Haigh, Parish Records, St. Luke's Church, Overton, West Yorkshire.

13   'Herbert Howden', *A Parish at War*, Accounts by Hilary Haigh, Parish Records, St. Luke's Church, Overton, West Yorkshire.

14   'Bernard and Herbert Howden', *A Parish at War*, Accounts by Hilary Haigh, Parish Records, St. Luke's Church, Overton, West Yorkshire.

the most dangerous of the anaerobic infections. This initial assessment was vital. A label, known as a 'specification tally' and looking very like a luggage label, was attached to a patient's uniform, informing clinicians further down the line what type of wound he had and what treatment he had received. The process by which information was communicated became more effective as the war progressed. By 1917, even if their wounds were concealed under heavy bandages and blankets, patients with the most severe and critical conditions could be recognised very quickly from the red borders on their labels.[15]

From the regimental aid post a patient would be taken by motor ambulance to a casualty clearing station where a range of treatments could be mobilized. Dehydration and haemorrhage meant that many required urgent treatment for so-called 'wound shock' before they were fit to undergo surgery. Fluid was pumped into the subcutaneous tissues beneath armpits and groins from large syringes through wide-bore needles, and stimulants were given into the muscles of the upper arm, thigh or buttock. In theatre, the patient's wounds were carefully debrided – a process of removing any infected, inflamed or dead tissue – and then packed with antiseptic-soaked dressings. From the spring of 1915 onwards antiseptic wound irrigation was the treatment of choice for most patients. A complex apparatus consisting of a glass bottle and glass and rubber tubing permitted the wound to be irrigated with fresh antiseptic every few hours, effectively flushing any lingering bacteria out of the wound. A range of antiseptic treatments was adopted, and, by 1915, these were causing some controversy, with different surgeons adhering to different approaches.[16]

John Schooling died at a CCS in Merville, about 40 miles from the front lines on 10 May, 1917. John had been born in Peckham in 1896, and appears to have travelled north to Yorkshire in order to find work in the mining industry. At the time of his enlistment, he was lodging with a Mr. and Mrs Isaac Parrott of Wichentree Hall, Sandy Lane, Middlestown and working at the Caphouse Pit,

15   Christine E. Hallett, *Nurses of Passchendaele: Caring for the Wounded of the Ypres Campaigns*, 1914-1918 (Barnsley, Pen and Sword Books, 2017)

16   Hallett, *Containing Trauma*; Hallett, Christine E., "Intelligent interest in their own affairs": The First World War, the *British Journal of Nursing* and the pursuit of nursing knowledge' in d'Antonio, P., Fairman, J. & Whelan, J. (eds.) *Routledge Handbook on the Global History of Nursing* (London & New York, Routledge, 2013): 95-113; Hallett, Veiled Warriors

Denby Grange Colliery. He served with the Army Cyclist Corps, a section of the army that provided support services, including message-carrying and trench-holding duties. He appears to have been wounded by a shrapnel shell, and was evacuated to Merville, an important medical centre in a strategic town, close to a railhead, where several CCSs were located. He is buried in the Merville Communal Cemetery Extension.[17]

Many soldiers were wounded on more than one occasion during the war. Ernest Froggatt, who had, like John Schooling, been working at Denby Grange Colliery - before enlisting during a recruiting meeting in April 1915 - was severely gassed on two separate occasions Each time, he had been moved down the line through regimental aid posts and CCSs to base hospitals, before being returned to active service. Treatment for gas injuries required close one-to-one nursing care. Drift gases such as chlorine, phosgene and bromine caused severe damage to patients' lungs and eyes, whilst later innovations, such as mustard gas and lewisite (which could be shot into trenches via gas shells) caused even more severe damage and could also burn the skin and gut. Patients were enabled to breathe by nurses who carefully positioned them, either on their sides, to drain fluid from the lungs, or propped in a sitting position to assist greater lung expansion. Oxygen was administered, if available; and patients' eyes were swabbed at two-hourly intervals. These patients were completely debilitated by the gas poisoning, and required total care: feeding, washing, toileting and re-positioning to prevent pressure sores.[18] Ernest recovered twice from gas damage, and survived two and a half years of war, only to die of wounds sustained during the German spring advance of 1918. He was killed at the Second Battle of Kemmel Ridge on 25 April 1918. Having survived two and a half years of war, he was still only 20 years old when he died. Ernest Froggett is commemorated at the Tyne Cot Memorial near Passchendaele.[19]

---

17   'John Schooling', *A Parish at War*, Accounts by Hilary Haigh, Parish Records St Luke's Church, Overton, West Yorkshire.

18   Hallett, Christine, E., '"This fiendish mode of warfare": nursing the victims of gas poisoning in the First World War', in Brooks, Jane & Hallett, Christine (eds.) *One Hundred Years of Wartime Nursing Practices* (Manchester, Manchester University Press, 2015)

19   'Ernest Froggett', *A Parish at War*, Accounts by Hilary Haigh, Parish Records, St. Luke's Church, Overton, West Yorkshire.

CCSs expanded as the war progressed. By 1917 a CCS could house several hundred beds in tented or hutted wards. Here patients' conditions were stabilised before they were moved further down the line. Some of the more severely wounded were kept in CCS wards for several weeks. Most, however, were moved rapidly 'down the line' to free-up space for new patients. CCSs were located close to railheads so that patients could be easily loaded onto the ambulance trains that would take them to large general hospitals at military bases in centres such as Etaples, Boulogne, Le Havre and Rouen.[20]

Like other elements of the lines of evacuation, ambulance trains were introduced fairly rapidly during the last five months of 1914 and the winter and spring of 1915. At first, the carriages of existing French passenger trains were hastily converted into makeshift hospital wards. Existing seating was retained in some carriages for 'sitting cases', whilst in wards for the most seriously wounded it was replaced with several rows of bunks in which patients could receive all the care and treatment they might be given in a normal hospital ward. Once it became clear that patients would need to be moved quite long distances from the 'zone of the armies' to bases many miles away, both private philanthropists and railway companies funded the rapid construction of purpose-built hospital trains, which were then shipped-out to France.[21]

Patients could spend anything from 6 to 36 hours on a hospital train, depending on how busy the railway lines were. Ambulance trains were always given the lowest priority, and, during large assaults, would experience frequent waits while soldiers, ammunition and supplies were brought up the line. Most of the fundamental nursing care for the wounded in ambulance trains was offered by medical orderlies of the Royal Army Medical Corps. Ambulance trains could consist of as many as 20 carriages, and most had only two or three fully-trained nurses, who, like the medical officers moved from carriage-to-carriage offering expert care and attention. Considering the seriousness of the conditions of many patients, it seems surprising that very few died en-route to the base. In spite of their desire to remove patients from CCSs and free beds for new casualties, medical officers and nurses evaluated patients for transfer very carefully, knowing

---

20   Hallett, *Nurses of Passchendaele*
21   Anonymous, *Ambulance Trains*, (York, National Railway Museum, 2016-2018)

that the train-journey – even in a hospital bunk – and with fully-trained nurses and doctors on hand – a patient on-board an ambulance train would be under considerable stress.[22]

On reaching the base, a patient would be transferred via motor ambulance to a general hospital, where more complex surgery could be performed, and wounds could be stabilised. Patients with infectious diseases such as trench fever, diphtheria or influenza were nursed in medical wards away from the surgical patients with wounds – although some patients, suffering from both infectious fevers and serious wounds, had to be carefully placed where they could receive expert attention without the risk that they might infect other vulnerable patients. At first established entirely under canvas, base hospitals increased in size as the war progressed and worn-out tentage was gradually replaced with wooden huts which offered greater shelter from the northern European weather, which, in winter months could be surprisingly harsh. After 1916, huts began to be seen as essential to protect patients and personnel from flying shrapnel; base hospitals were increasingly likely to be bombarded from the air by bombing raids by specially-designed Gothas, each of which could carry up to 500 kilograms of shells.[23]

If a patient survived long enough to be treated at a regimental aid post, a CCS, on board an ambulance train and then at a base hospital, he was likely to survive his injuries. Some were, however, unlucky. Patients with deep wounds located close to arteries could suffer sudden, catastrophic haemorrhages. Others had intractable wound-infections that no number of operations or antiseptic treatments could eradicate. Robert Stubbs was one such unfortunate patient. He had been born in Blackpool, but his parents appear to have moved to Horbury, close to Wakefield, in 1894, and it was here that Robert was baptised. He later moved to Ossett, where he began work at the Co-operative store as a butcher. He married Sarah Lydia Metcalfe in St Luke's Church on 15 February, 1915, and the couple then moved back to Robert's home town of Blackpool. Robert joined the 3rd Battalion of the Coldstream Guards in October 1916. It is possible that he had been unwilling to serve in the armed forces: he joined the army just after

---

22   On the care of patients on ambulance trains see: Hallett, *Nurses of Passchendaele*.

23   On the bombing of hospitals, see: Hallett, *Veiled Warriors*; Hallett, *Nurses of Passchendaele*.

the date at which all married men became subject to conscription in the autumn of 1916.[24]

On 30 July 1917, Sarah Stubbs received a telegram informing her that her husband had been wounded on the Ypres Salient and had been evacuated to a CCS. One arm and one leg had been badly damaged and it appears that Robert had sustained one of the most dangerous injuries of the war – fractured femur – a condition that had been associated with a very high mortality rate prior to the introduction of the Thomas Splint in 1916, and was still seen as an injury requiring very rapid intervention. Robert was moved down the line by ambulance train to Wimereux, where the matron of his base hospital wrote to his wife to let her know that his leg had been amputated. Another telegram followed soon after, to notify Sarah that Robert was dangerously ill. He died on 10 August, 1917, at the age of 22. His widow later received a letter from the hospital chaplain, who informed her that Robert had borne 'his pain and sufferings most bravely, like a true soldier', adding, 'I was able to be with him in his last moments, and he was quite content to go to his saviour… He was perfectly conscious and received the sacrament with great devotion… In beautiful sunshine and under a clear blue sky, his coffin, covered with white flowers was laid in the grave'.[25]

Many patients were treated at base hospitals until their wounds were entirely healed and they were deemed fit for return to a rest camp and then back into an active military unit. More severely damaged patients – particularly those whose wounds were likely to take months to heal and those who were so severely damaged that they could never be returned to the front lines – were loaded onto hospital ships and brought back across the English Channel to hospitals at home. Upon arrival at the channel ports, they were transferred to ambulance trains and taken to so-called 'territorial hospitals' in large towns and cities, or to the auxiliary hospitals that were, effectively the outposts of these large general hospitals. Many were sent first to a Territorial hospital to be evaluated and treated, and then

---

24   Robert Stubbs', *A Parish at War*, Accounts by Hilary Haigh, Parish Records, St. Luke's Church, Overton, West Yorkshire.

25   'Robert Stubbs', *A Parish at War*, Accounts by Hilary Haigh, Parish Records, St. Luke's Church, Overton, West Yorkshire. The quotation is from: *Wakefield Express* (18 August, 1917), 6

moved to an auxiliary hospital for rehabilitation. A range of buildings were used to house auxiliary hospitals – including the stately homes of the aristocracy and gentry.[26]

A severely wounded man – such as one who had, for example, suffered one or more amputation or a severe chest, abdominal, face or head injury – might spend several months, even years, receiving surgical treatment before his wounds were completely healed. Even at this point, some men died of their wounds. One particularly sad story was that of Percy Rooke Littlewood, who died after the war's end on 13 December, 1918 at the Bellahouston Red Cross Hospital in Glasgow. Percy had been baptised at St Luke's Church on 2 March, 1885. In his mid-teens he was apprenticed to a mason, but the work appears not to have suited him and in the 1911 Census, he is recorded as an asylum attendant at Prestwich Hospital in Manchester. He enlisted in the Leicestershire Regiment while working in Manchester, and was wounded in action on 30 September 1918. His knee was shattered by an explosive bullet, and it took 12 hours for him to be rescued from no-man's-land by stretcher bearers, and. By the time he reached a hospital, his wound – which undoubtedly involved severe and complex damage to the knee joint - would, most probably, have been very badly infected. He was taken to a French hospital, before being transferred to a British CCS, from which he was evacuated 'down the line' in October. At Bellahouston he is likely to have undergone several operations – possibly repeat amputations, in a series of attempts to arrest the infection. But these were to no avail and he eventually died, several weeks after his return to Britain. His body was brought back to Middlestown, where it was buried with military honours in Thornhill Churchyard.[27]

The 'long, long trail' which brought wounded men back to Britain from the horrors of the First World War's battlefields was a remarkable logistical achievement. The development of carefully-placed hospitals and the supply of motor ambulances and ambulance trains enabled senior military surgeons and nurses to develop and implement new life-saving treatments such as wound

---

26   Hallett, *Veiled Warriors.*
27   'Percy Rooke Littlewood', *A Parish at War,* Accounts by Hilary Haigh, Parish Records, St. Luke's Church, Overton, West Yorkshire.

irrigation, the surgical removal of infected tissue, and techniques to restore the health of severely gassed casualties. Yet, in spite of the best efforts of what was, effectively, an 'army' of healers, hundreds of thousands of British men died before they could reach the end of the trail and return to their longed-for homes.

WAR
MEMORIALS

War Memorials at Midgley, St Andrew's, St Luke's and Trinty Methodists

THE MEN WHO
DID NOT RETURN

Christine Hewitt, Steve Wilson
and Hilary Haigh

THE FIRST WORLD War left an indelible mark on the Parish of Middlestown with Netherton. At least thirty-five young men from the parish perished and many have no known grave. Many more served and returned, some of them wounded and disabled. This chapter will tell the story of those who did not return.

The war started on 4 August 1914 and by the end of October two local men, Private Thomas Copley Jackson from Midgley and Private Harold Davies from Middlestown, had been killed.

1914

Thomas Copley Jackson was born on 18 January 1895, the third child of John and Mary Jackson, both aged 31 years. Thomas was baptised on 10 November 1895 in Bretton Chapel, in the parish of Silkstone and Sandal.

By 1911 Thomas was living with his family in Windy Bank, Midgley. His father was working at Earnshaw's wood yard and Thomas was working in the pit as a coal mine rope ender.

Soon after war was declared, Thomas enlisted in the King's Own Yorkshire Light Infantry in Pontefract and served as a Private in the 2nd Battalion, with the regimental number 10891.

Within three months Thomas was dead, aged 19 years, killed during the bitter fighting during the Battle of La Bassee which took place between 10 October and 2 November 1914.

The 2nd King's Own Yorkshire Light Infantry were part of 13th Brigade of the 5th Division, which was in the part of the battlefield between Neuve Chapelle and Givenchy.

On the 26 October the Germans launched an attack to capture Neuve Chapelle, and eventually succeeded after heavy fighting; however the Germans actually withdrew from the village a couple of days later.

Earnshaw's Wood Yard

The following paragraphs are extracts from the War Diary of 2 KOYLI for the day on which Thomas was killed:

26th October 1914. Early morning. Very heavy shell firing on our trenches today from early morning. D Company's trench was badly broken up for 40 yards. Men were buried alive. Capt. R W S STANTON was wounded in the thigh by a piece of shell. The shelling consisted chiefly of so-called "Jack Johnsons" the 738 lb Lyddite shell. 17 men were killed and about 40 wounded.

Thomas Copley Jackson's body was not found and his name is carved on the memorial to the missing at Le Touret as well as on the memorials at Midgley and in St Andrew's Church, Netherton.

Three days later, on 29 October 1914, Private Harold Davies of the Coldstream Guards was killed.

Private Harold Davies (Coldstream Guards), of Sandy-lane, Middlestown, who, as reported in our last issue, was killed near Ypres.

Private Harold Davies was born in Thornhill in about 1895. His father, William Thomas, was born in Staffordshire and his mother Alice hailed from Newmarket. Their sons Harold and Ernest were born in Thornhill and their daughter was born in Middlestown. By 1911 the family was living in Sandy Lane, Middlestown and William Thomas was employed as a Water Inspector Road Foreman for the Rural District Council and Harold, then aged 15 years old, was also working for the Rural District Council, assisting with a road engine.

Harold was a member of Middlestown Athletic Club. He enlisted in the Coldstream Guards at the outbreak of war, and was part of the British Expeditionary Force. The Coldstream Guards, as part of 1st (Guards) Brigade, 1st division, were among the first British soldiers to enter France, and his battalion arrived there on the 14 August 1914. These were the men of the British Expeditionary Force who became known at the 'Old Contemptibles'.

Harold was missing between 29 October and 2 November 1914 and is thought to have been killed on 29 October 1914; he was 19 years old.

The 1st Battalion, Coldstream Guards had relieved 2nd Battalion, Yorkshire Regiment in trenches close to the Nieuwe Kruiseecke crossroads at Gheluvelt village when the enemy attacked in large numbers on October 29th 1914. On the 27th October 1914 the battalion arrived at Gheluvelt, south-east of Ypres.

The battalion war diary of the 1st Coldstream Guards is brief and lacks detail, but the entry for the day of Harold Davies' death is as follows:

Oct 29th 1914: An attack by the Germans of which notice was received was beaten off at 5.30 am. in dense mist, but was successful further

Remembered with Honour
Zantvoorde British Cemetery

S. at crossroads E.S.E of Gheluvelt; the result being that the battalion trenches were almost immediately afterwards attacked from the right rear. A retirement appears to have been ordered and a small portion of the battalion re-formed covering a battery of the Royal Field Artillery.

At night the battalion was withdrawn and bivouacked in woods W. of Gheluvelt in Brigade Reserve. The official History of The Battalion states:

On 29th Oct 1914, at Gheluvelt, the 1st Battalion suffered such casualties that it had no officers left and only 80 men. Four days later, after reinforcement, it had once more been reduced to no officers and 120 men only.

His personal effects were handed to his father, William Thomas Davies and Harold is commemorated in ZANTVOORDE British Cemetery in Belgium and on the war memorial in St Luke's Church, Overton.

1915

The year 1915 saw four more families bereaved as Private Willie Taylor, Sergeant Harry Moxon, Private Wilfrid Hooper and Private Frederick William Gill were killed between the months of March and September.

Private Willie Taylor of the Royal Marine Light Infantry (RMLI), aged 29 years, was one of the 22 Royal Marines who died during the first day of the RMLI landing at the Gallipoli beaches on 4 March 1915.

Willie was the son of Friend and Eliza Taylor. He was baptised in St Luke's Church, Middlestown on 9 April 1886 and by 1911, like his father, Willie was working as a coal hewer in the pit. The family lived in a two-roomed house in Kaye's Yard, Overton.

When war broke out, Willie enlisted and became a private in the RMLI, (perhaps along with the other young men from the parish who were involved in the defence of Antwerp but then held in Holland as internees, as described above).

In addition to their usual stations aboard ship, Royal Marines were part of the Royal Naval Division which landed in Belgium in 1914 to help defend Antwerp and later served on the Western Front in the trenches as well as in the amphibious landing at Gallipoli in which Willie Taylor took part:

AN OVERTON MAN MISSING.

The following is a copy of a letter received by Mr. and Mrs. Friend Taylor, Kaye's yard, Overton:—

"Record Office R.N.D.,
74, Victoria Street, S.W.
7th March, 1915.

"I regret to inform you that your son, Private Willie Taylor 8121, who was serving with the Royal Navy Division in the Eastern Mediterranean Sea, is reported as missing, after operations on the 4th March.—I am your obedient servant,

A. RANDALL WELLS,
Lieutenant, R.N.V.R.

Wakefield Express 13 March 1915 p9

4 March 1915 8:30 am, Plymouth Battalion landed one company each at Kum Kale and Sedd-el-Bahr, to cover the demolition of Turkish guns by raiding parties.

Sedd-el-Bahr company re-embarks at 2.30pm, Kum Kale at 7.15pm. Operations successful, at cost of 22 dead and 22 wounded.

Initially reported missing in a letter dated 7 March 1915, Willie Taylor's parents, Mr and Mrs Friend Taylor of Kaye's Yard, Overton, eventually heard the news that their son was one of the dead. He is commemorated on panel 2-7 of the Helles Memorial in Turkey and on the War Memorial in St Luke's Church, Overton.

Less than a week after Willie Taylor was killed, on 12 March 1915, the parish lost another of its young men, Sergeant Harry Moxon of the 2nd Battalion, Yorkshire Regiment.

Born in 1886 in Kexborough, Yorkshire, to George Peace Moxon, aged 37 and Emma (nee Challenger), aged 35. Harry Moxon had four brothers and five sisters.

He was baptised in Darton All Saints Church on 14 November 1886 and continued to live in Kexborough in his early years, but by 1901 the family had moved to Midgley and Harry was working with his father on the family farm, Pot House Farm.

By 1911 Harry, a 24 year old single man, was still living at home and working on his father's farm, although as he had served in the army, he was a reservist. The

following account of his rejoining the army appears in Hubert Moxon Earnshaw's *The Village of Midgley Book 2*

...Harry's Aunt Bertha recalled as though it were yesterday, her brother Harry Moxon, who was a reservist, getting his calling up papers whilst he was working on the farm, Pot House. He was so pleased to be off to the fight that he kept throwing his cap into the air several times for joy, as he went over the fields taking a short cut to Little London and Netherton, to get to the station at Horbury. Poor Harry, who was such a fine man in his prime, was sent to the heavy fighting about Christmas, became a Sergeant and was killed by a sniper's bullet whilst taking someone else's place in the front rank.

(*The Village of Midgley Book 2* by Hubert Moxon Earnshaw).

Harry kept in touch with his family and some of his experiences in the army are set out in his surviving letters, published above.

During the Battle of Neuve Chapelle, 10 to 12 March 1915, the 2nd Battalion of the Yorkshire Regiment (Green Howards) were part of the 7th Division, 21st Brigade.

Neuve Chapelle is a small village located roughly midway between Bethune and Lille, and is around 20 miles south of Ypres. This first British set-piece attack of the War was planned here early in 1915 by Douglas Haig, at that time in command of the First Army. The intention was initially to capture the German lines in this German salient, then the village itself, and then drive through onto the nearby Aubers Ridge, where the high ground had the usual strategic value. If this was achieved, the enemy's lines of communication between La Bassee and Lille could also be disrupted.

However, as the days progressed, the attack was held up and the Germans, who had been taken by surprise, were able to bring up reinforcements and mount counter attacks over the next two days, and although reports of operations cover the 10 - 14 March, the Battle is officially considered as just the three days of 10 March to 12 March. The War Diary records that on the morning of 12 March 1915

2/Yorks (Green Howards) repulse advance with M/Guns

2/RSF broken through but 2/Beds counter-attack and force withdrawal with losses

BRETTON WEST SERGEANT KILLED.

Mr. and Mrs. G. P. Moxon, of Pot House Farm, Bretton, have received news from the War Office that their son, Sergeant Harry Moxon, was killed in action during the severe fighting of the last few weeks. Sergeant Moxon had seen a good deal of fighting, and his letters home gave graphic descriptions of the murderous warfare, and wanton destruction of the German soldiers. The news of his death caused a painful sensation in the village, as he was a popular young man, and was well respected by all who knew him.

Wakefield Express 1 April 1915

A SERVICE "IN MEMORIAM."

On Sunday afternoon at Midgley U.M. Chapel, a service was held in memory of Sergt. Harry Moxon, 3rd Batt. Yorkshire Regiment, who was killed in action on the morning of the 12th March, at Neuve Chapelle. The chapel was well filled. At the outset the "Dead March" (Saul) was played by the organist (Mr. George Earnshaw), the congregation standing. Mr. Wm. Challenger (Elsecar) gave a sympathetic address, based on the words "I have fought the good fight" (II. Tim. r. 6). "O God, our help in ages past," "A few more years shall roll," "What are these arrayed in white," and "For ever with the Lord" were sung. Amongst the congregation were members of the Clayton West Ambulance Association, of which the deceased had been an active member. Much sympathy is felt for Moxon's parents and family. The deceased was very well known and respected.

Wakefield Express 15 April 1915

War Memorial, West Bretton

The casualty figures for the British were around 3,500 killed and 8,500 wounded. German casualty figures are more difficult to come by, but must have also run into thousands. 28 year-old Sergeant Harry Moxon was one of those killed in the battle.

Harry is named on the Bretton village war memorial, on the roadside war memorial in Midgley, on the earlier but lost memorial in the United Methodist Church in Midgley and on panel 12 of the Le Touret Memorial in France. The articles opposite about Harry were published in the *Wakefield Express*.

Private Wilfrid Hooper
1/4 Bn KOYLI
2934

Wakefield Express
18 September 1915 p6

Private Wilfrid Hooper was the son of Joe and Anne Hooper of Grosvenor Terrace, Middlestown.

A keen athlete, Wilfrid was a founding member of Middlestown Athletic Club and along with other members of the Club, Harry Bedford, Leonard Shires, Eddie Schofield and Cyril Froggatt, Wilfrid enlisted in the 1/4 Battalion of the King's Own Yorkshire Light Infantry (KOYLI) in Wakefield in November 1914.

1/4 and 1/5 KOYLI arrived in France on 12/13 April 1915. On the 15 May 1915, the formation became 148th Brigade, 49th (West Riding) Division.

In July 1915 1/4 KOYLI were in trenches close to the Yser Canal, south of Ypres, where they remained for some weeks. On the 2 September 1915 they relieved 1/5 KOYLI in the front line of trenches.

THE DEATH OF A MIDDLESTOWN SOLDIER.
RESPECTED BY ALL HIS COMRADES.

Mr. and Mrs. Joe Hooper, Grosvenor-terrace, Middlestown, have this week been informed of the death of their eldest son, Private Wilfrid Hooper, and they have received several letters of sympathy from members of the battalion, including one from the Commander, Lieut.-Colonel Hastegrave. Rev. J. Sidney Hobson, Wesleyan Chaplain, in the course of his letter says:—

"Private Hooper and several others of the same regiment were hit by a German shell about 3 o'clock on Monday afternoon, the 6th inst., and your dear son was killed instantaneously. He was buried last night at a farm near the trenches, though for some reasons I was not sent for to the service. I understand that another chaplain performed the last rites on the body of your brave lad. . . It is with some consolation to know that your son was a true hero, and that in his death he had absolutely no pain."

Bandsman Herman Bowers (Netherton), stretcher-bearer, who was in the same company as deceased and an old friend, says:—

"I have always been proud of his friendship. He met his death doing his duty for his King and country. He was on a working party with a few more men, when a shell dropped and killed him and a sergeant named Blacker, from Horbury, who was with the same party. I am sure no one could have been more respected or more liked by his comrades, and we all feel this death very much."

Lieutenant E. W. Moorhouse, in the course of his letter, said Hooper was one of his best men, and a favourite with all. Much sympathy is felt for Mr. and Mrs. Hooper in the loss of their son, who previous to joining the Colours at the beginning of the war was employed as a clerk at the Denby Grange Collieries' offices. He was held in high esteem by all who knew him. He was also a member of the Middlestown Athletic Club, and was captain of the football section. He was a clever right wing forward, and as an all round athlete his equal would have been hard to find. He was also a playing member of the Denby Grange Colliery Cricket Club, and last year held the position of secretary. He would have been 31 years of age to-day (Saturday) had he lived. The athletic club, of which deceased was one of the founders, has now over 20 members serving their country.

The War Diary for 1/4 KOYLI on the 6 September tells us: *Enemy shelled front line at intervals. Casualties 3 killed, 3 wounded, 2 sick.*

One of those killed was 20 year-old Private Wilfrid Hooper; he was 20 years old. The obituary over the page was published in the *Wakefield Express*.

He is buried in Bard Cottage Cemetery, Belgium; the epitaph on his gravestone reads 'He put Duty First'. Wilfrid is also commemorated on the war memorial in St Luke's Church, Overton.

Less than three weeks later, on 27 September 1915, Wilfrid's cousin, Private Frederick William Gill of the Machine Gun Section, 9th Battalion, King's Own Yorkshire Light Infantry, was killed in the Battle of Loos.

Frederick William was the Son of John Thomas and Elizabeth Wilson Gill. He was baptised on 13 July 1887 in the parish of Sandal and lived there with his family until his marriage in 1911.

Frederick William's father, John Thomas Gill, was a Mail Contractor, sub-postmaster and carriage proprietor, who had been born in Pontefract; his wife Elizabeth was born in Houghton-on-Hill, Leicestershire and their first son, John Edward Gill, was born in Linslade, Bucks, an indication, perhaps of the peripatetic nature of John Thomas's business. Their four further children, however, were all born in Sandal and their address in 1911 was Virginia Cottage, a five-roomed house.

Frederick William was a Joiner; he was 24 when on 21 January 1912 he married Dorris (sic) Wakefield, the 19 year old daughter of Charles William Wakefield, a fireman.

After their marriage, Frederick William and Dorris moved to Middlestown and lived in Wichentree Cottage, Sandy Lane. Frederick William was employed as a joiner at Denby Grange Collieries until he enlisted in the KOYLI 9th Battalion in Dewsbury.

The 9th Battalion, King's Own Yorkshire Light Infantry was raised at Pontefract in September 1914 as part of Kitchener's Third New Army and joined 64th Brigade, 21st Division. After initial training close to home they moved to Berkhamsted and then to Halton Park in October. They spent the winter in billets in Maidenhead from November and returned to Halton Park in April 1915. They moved to Witley for final training in August and proceeded to France in September 1915.

They marched across France and went straight into action in reserve of the British assault at Loos on the 26 of September, suffering heavy casualties, including 28 year-old Private Frederick William Gill, who was killed during the bitter fighting to take Hill 70 during the Battle of Loos on the 26/27 September 1915.

The battle on 26 September seems to have been even more difficult than the 25 September. This from Philip Warner's book *The Battle of Loos:*

"........At the start of the attack (25th) they (the Germans) had been surprised, but had contrived to retreat in reasonable order, taking their artillery with them. British Intelligence had calculated that at the best the Germans could rush no more than 5 Divisions to this sector during the first day of battle; in the event the Germans brought up nearly 7. These fresh troops busied themselves during the night with wiring the second position and siting machine guns. What had the day before been an incomplete trench system with, in many parts, a single strand of wire in front, now had a strong entanglement, well-staked, 4 feet high and 20 feet deep. When 21st (including the 9 KOYLI as part of 64 Brigade) and 24th Divisions were launched into the attack at 1100 on the 26th September they were advancing against uncut wire and undamaged positions (you must also remember the drastic shortage of shells on the Brit side), for there had been no preceding artillery bombardment, furthermore they had no gas or smoke to cover them, but were expected to advance over open ground, littered with the dead and wounded of the previous day.

......21 Division were ordered to deploy on a thousand yard frontage between Fosse 7 (on the Bethune-Lens road) and the Vermelles-Loos track (it was not a proper road). This would make them beginning the day on the western edge of Loos and moving through to about a mile SE of that town.

The Wakefield Express gave the following account of Frederick William Gill's death:

Frederick William's effects went to Dorris, his sole legatee and, as well as in St Luke's Church, Middlestown, he is remembered on the Loos memorial as well as on the war memorial in St Luke's Church, Overton.

> GILL, Pte. Frederick William, 15600. 9th Bn. King's Own Yorkshire Light Inf. 27th Sept., 1915. Age 28. Son of Mr. and Mrs. John Thomas Gill, of Bootham Cottage, York; husband of Dorris Gill, of 43, Albert Villas, Major St., Thornes, Wakefield, Yorks.

SANDAL AND MIDDLESTOWN JOINER KILLED IN ACTION.

HIT BY A SNIPER.

The news has been received of the death of Private Frederick William Gill, of the Machine Gun Section, 9th Batt. K.O.Y.L.I., a son of Mr. Gill, of the Post Office, Sandal, and who lived at Wichentree Cottage, Middlestown, with his wife and child.

Gill was a joiner at the Denby Grange Collieries, and he was highly respected by all who knew him. Before going to Middlestown he lived most of his time in Sandal. At the outbreak of hostilities Private Gill, who was 28 years of age, joined the colours, and eventually went to France. On the 24th Sept. he wrote a letter to his wife saying he was then only a few miles behind the firing-line, and was on his way to the trenches. The sad news of his death, which took place on the 26th, came as a great shock to all who knew him. The widow received the intimation in the following letter, written on the 27th by Sergeant Winwood:—

"Dear Mrs. Gill.—I am very sorry to inform you that your husband was killed by a sniper while bringing ammunition to the guns. He had no pain, as he died straight away. You had a husband which you can always be proud of, as he died doing his duty for his King and Country. All the officers and all his chums were very sorry to lose him, as he was a good chap, always willing to do anything he was asked. We all sympathise with you in your great loss of such a good husband."

Wakefield Express 9 October 1915

Loos Memorial

1916

The year 1916 saw twelve local men killed in the war, the highest death toll of the parish in the conflict. Many of these men took part in the Battle of the Somme, which started on 1 July 1916 and lasted until November 1916, but Lieutenant Cecil Clarke Bedford of the 1st Manchesters was killed in Mesopotamia on 8 March 1916 although his brother, Private William Henry Bedford of the 1/4 King's Own Yorkshire Light Infantry died on 14 July 1916 of wounds sustained on the first day of the Battle of the Somme.

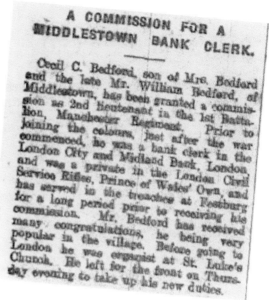

A COMMISSION FOR A MIDDLESTOWN BANK CLERK.

Cecil C. Bedford, son of Mrs. Bedford and the late Mr. William Bedford, of Middlestown, has been granted a commission as 2nd lieutenant in the 1st Battalion, Manchester Regiment. Prior to joining the colours, just after the war commenced, he was a bank clerk in the London City and Midland Bank, London, and was a private in the London Civil Service Rifles, Prince of Wales' Own, and has served in the trenches at Festubury for a long period prior to receiving his commission. Mr. Bedford has received many congratulations, he being very popular in the village. Before going to London he was organist at St. Luke's Church. He left for the front on Thursday evening to take up his new duties.

Wakefield Express 31 July 1915

2nd Lieutenant Cecil Clarke Bedford and Private Harry Bedford were the sons of builder William Henry and his wife Mary Bedford, of Cliff Cottage, Cross Road, Middlestown.

Both boys were baptised in St Luke's Church and attended St Luke's School; Cecil attended Wakefield Academy in York Street before employment as a clerk with the London City and Midland Bank. Before moving to London, Cecil was organist at St Luke's and a Sunday School teacher as well as being Secretary of Horbury Golf Club. Cecil was the only officer among the men from the parish who died in the war.

On 8 January 1916, the 1st Battalion, Manchester Regiment arrived in Basra, Mesopotamia (now Iraq) re-equipped and proceeded to Shaik Sa'ad. They were attached to the 7th Brigade with the intention of relieving the Siege of Kut. On the 19 January, the brigade advanced west along the River Tigris, fighting small actions as they went along. On the 20th the main attack on the Hannah position started but the Manchesters played little part in it, being employed on piquet and reserve.

On 5 February, the battalion was in trenches on the south bank of Tigris with little other than patrol duties; a draft of 131 men was received.

In March 1916, the battalion was in trenches at Abu Roman and a new draft of 202 men was received on 4 March. On the 7 March the battalion was part of the attack on the Dujalah redoubt, advancing across a front of 400 yards; they came under heavy fire from the Sinn Aftar redoubt and cross fire from supporting trenches. They gained a footing in the redoubt and took two trenches, however with bombs running out and under heavy counterattack from the left flank, they were forced to retire with many casualties (172 killed or missing, 288 wounded), including 25 year old 2nd Lt. Cecil Clarke Bedford.

MIDDLESTOWN OFFICER KILLED IN MESOPOTAMIA.

AN OLD WAKEFIELD ACADEMY BOY.

The sad news was received in Middlestown on Tuesday of the death in action of Second-Lieutenant Cecil Clark Bedford, aged 25, third son of the late Mr. William Henry Bedford and of Mrs. Bedford, Cliffe Cottage. The first intimation was in a telegram received by his mother, stating that he had been missing since March 8th, and later in the evening, his elder brother, Mr. Ernest Bedford, received the following telegram from the War Office :—"Sorry to say Lieutenant C. C. Bedford was killed in action on March 8th in Mesopotamia. Lord Kitchener expresses his deepest sympathy."

Much sympathy is felt in the village with the bereaved mother and family, as deceased was a well-known and highly-respected young man. He was educated at the Wakefield Academy, and afterwards he was a clerk in Mr. Pollard's colliery engineer's office at Wakefield. Subsequently he became a clerk in the London City and Midland Bank, being drafted to Holmfirth. Later he was transferred to Heckmondwike, and after passing a difficult examination he was transferred to the head office in Threadneedle-street, London.

He was a clever player on the piano, forte and organ, and when living at Middlestown he was the organist at St. Luke's Church and also a Sunday school teacher for a number of years. He was secretary and a prominent member of the Horbury and District Golf Club. Whilst in London he several times played the organ at the services at St. Martin's Church.

On Sept. 1st, 1914, deceased joined the Prince of Wales' Civil Service Rifles as a private, and on March 17th, 1915, he went to France. On June 15th he went to a cadet school, and after gaining his commission as second-lieutenant he was transferred to the 1st Manchester Regiment, leaving on the 8th December last for Egypt.

His brother, Private William H. Bedford, is with the 4th K.O.Y.L.I. in France

Wakefield Express 18 March 1916

He is commemorated on the Basra Memorial and in the St Oswald war memorial window in St Luke's Church which is dedicated to the memory of Cecil and his brother, William Henry (Harry) Bedford.

Cecil's brother Harry was wounded in the Somme offensive of 1 July 1916 and died on the 14 July 1916 in hospital in Rouen; he was 21 years old. Before enlisting, Harry, a former pupil at Ossett Grammar School, was employed as a clerk at

MIDDLESTOWN WIDOW'S
SACRIFICE.

TWO SONS KILLED IN ACTION.

There was much regret in Middlestown on Saturday, when it became known that Private William Henry (Harry) Bedford had succumbed to wounds. He was 21 years of age, and the youngest son of the late Mr. W. H. and of Mrs. Bedford, Cliffe Cottage.

Deceased was educated at the Middlestown St. Luke's and Ossett Grammar Schools and afterwards until joining the forces he was employed as a clerk at the Denby Grange Collieries. He was a prominent member of the Middlestown Athletic Club, being a very good wrestler, and also a playing member of the Denby Grange Colliery Cricket Club. He was an active member of St. Luke's Church and also a communicant.

Deceased was a brother of the late Lieut. Cecil C. Bedford, who was killed in action in March in Mesopotamia. Much sympathy is felt with Mrs. Bedford and family in the loss of her second son. Pte. Bedford enlisted in October, 1914, and went out to France on April 16th, 1915, and was home on leave in November last, just at the same time as his late brother was on his last leave after gaining his commission. Pte. Bedford served for a time in the trenches and afterwards was transferred to the trench mortar battery in which he served until being severely wounded.

Messages were received by the family from the Matron of Rouen Hospital almost daily stating how serious a condition he was in, and a telegram was received on Saturday noon stating that he died at five minutes past twelve on Friday morning. The following letter was received on Tuesday from the Rev. Dr. Rickards, S.C.F. Rouen Base:—

"Dear madam,—It is with regret that I inform you of the death at 12.5 this morning in this hospital of your son, Pte. W. H. Bedford. He came here some days ago severely wounded in the left thigh and left arm, and in spite of all that could be done for him his strength gradually failed. It has been my privilege constantly to attend him since he has been here, and I was able to administer the Blessed Sacrament to him only a day or two ago. He bore his sickness patiently and met the end nobly. It is seldom one meets a better patient, and in your sorrow I am sure that the realization of this must be a comfort to you. His funeral will take place to-morrow in the cemetery of St. Sever, Rouen, and I will ask the Grave Regulation Commission to send you a photograph of the grave."

Wakefield Express 22 July 1916

Denby Grange Colliery and was a member of Middlestown Athletic Club. He is buried in St Sever cemetery and is commemorated with his brother in the St Oswald war memorial window in St Luke's Church.

Mary Bedford, already a widow, lost two of her sons in 1916.

Lance Corporal Joseph Dunn
12 Battalion KOYLI
12/128

Like William Henry Bedford, Lance Corporal Dunn was also a casualty of the Battle of the Somme.

Lance Corporal Dunn hailed from the Selby area but lived with his uncle, Joseph Pool at Mount Pleasant, Middlestown during the time he was employed at Denby Grange Colliery. When war came he enlisted in the 12th Battalion of the King's Own Yorkshire Light Infantry.

This Battalion's history dates from 5 September 1914 when the War Office authorised the West Yorkshire Coalowners' Association to raise a Miners' Battalion for the King's Own (Yorkshire Light Infantry).

After beginning its life at Leeds, the battalion trained first at Farnley Park, Otley and then at Burton Leonard, near Ripon. By this time it had been allocated to 31st Division as its pioneer battalion.

After completing its training in Yorkshire, the battalion moved to Fovant, Salisbury in October 1915 before embarking for Egypt on 6 December. After little more than two months in Egypt, the 12th KOYLI was ordered to France (landing at Marseilles on the 9 March 1916) to take part in the planned summer offensive on the Somme.

At zero hour (7:30am) on Saturday, 1 July 1916, whistles blew all along the British line to signal the beginning of the Somme offensive. 60,000 men, the first wave of the attack rose ungainly from their starting points and began to walk out into no-man's land.

Lance Corporal Joseph Dunn was killed in action on that day, in the attack on the village of Serre, carried out by the Army 31st Division, of which the 12th Battalion, KOYLI was an important part. The failure of 31st Division's attack at Serre in the face of overwhelming enemy artillery and machine gun fire is well-known. On the 94th Brigade front, two platoons from "A" Company of the 12th KOYLI followed the 12th York & Lancasters (Sheffield City Battalion) and 11th East Lancashires (Accrington Pals) into the attack; as many as four out of every five men from these two KOYLI platoons were wounded or killed.

Joseph Dunn's effects were left to William Pool, the sole legatee and a memorial service, attended by a large congregation, was held for him at St Luke's Church. The Vicar, Rev G. C. Hamilton, preached on the latter verses of Paul's Letter to the Thessalonians, Chapter Four and after the singing of 'Brief Life is Here our Portion', 'Days and Moments quickly flying', and 'O God of Love King of Peace' the Dead March in Saul was played on the organ by Mr Walter Balmforth:

Thiepval Memorial to the missing   *Wakefield Express* 2 September 1916

The Earnshaw family lost three members in the First World War. The first to die was **Private Fred Earnshaw,** 1364, of the 10th Battalion, Lincolnshire Regiment, who was killed on 1 July 1916, the first day of the Battle of the Somme; Rifleman Edward Earnshaw of the King's Royal Rifle Corps and Corporal Walter Earnshaw of the Duke of Wellington's (West Riding Regiment) were both killed on 17 September 1916. All three of these young men are commemorated on the Memorial of the Missing at Thiepval, France, as well as on the war memorials in St Andrew's Church, Netherton and the memorial at Midgley.

Born on 3 November 1895, the eldest child of Henry and Eliza Earnshaw of Woodland View, Midgley and grandson of William Earnshaw, Timber Merchant and his wife Martha of Midgley.

Fred was educated at St Andrew's School, Netherton, Ossett Grammar School and, like Lt Cecil Bedford, at the York Street Academy, Wakefield before employment as a draughtsman by Messrs Charles Roberts and Company, Horbury Bridge.

Fred enlisted in the 10th Battalion, Lincolnshire Regiment (Grimsby Chums) on 10 February 1915. On 15 December 1915 he visited St Andrew's Church School to tell the children about his experiences as a soldier:

Private Fred Earnshaw R.E., who, as a scholar attended the St Andrew's Day School in this village, is home for a week's furlough from the Trenches near Loos (France). He expressed a wish to visit this school and see the children at work and as a consequence he spent about half an hour this morning in the various class rooms. He modestly described some of his experiences in actual warfare.

15 December 1915. (*Netherton School Log Book*, WYAS, Wakefield)

On 1 July 1916, the first day of the Battle of the Somme, the section of the line held by the Grimsby Chums and their 101st Brigade comrades was at La Boiselle. Prior to attack, at 7.28am a large mine was exploded beneath the German line. The Chums were due to attack at 7.30am, but, unknown to the Battalion, the mine fell short of the German positions and during the two minute gap between the explosion and the "whistle" the enemy had the chance to set the machine guns.

The Chums were drawn up with A Company on the right, B Company on the left and C Company, opposite the crater, in the centre. D Company was in reserve for phase two. They advanced in four straight lines with no hesitation. It was a matter of moments before the first men fell, as the German mortars and machine guns opened up. Officers and men alike dropped to the ground as if the move was planned during training. Only a few men reached the German trenches, bombing for all they were worth, but in too few numbers and they had to retreat.

By 9am, D Company were sent into the attack, led by Major Vignoles, who was soon hit in the hand. Again, the attack broke up and the 10th Lincolns were left powerless to attack, lying in shell holes in no man's land in the baking sun. All were waiting for nightfall to be able to crawl back to their own lines for treatment. Several attempts to attack were made with the remnants of the Battalion on the 2 July and 3 July. When they were finally withdrawn and the roll was called, 15 Officers and 487 men (out of 1,000) had been killed, were missing or had been wounded. One of the dead was Private Fred Earnshaw; he was 20 years old.

It was some days before his death was recorded and his body was never found. Captain John Kennington wrote the following to Fred's parents:

'…it is with great sorrow that I write to inform you of the sad death of your son, Pvte. Fred Earnshaw. He was killed in action on the 1st inst. I should have written you before, but the official information has only just come to hand. It may be a little consolation to you to know that your son was held in high esteem in his platoon. He was a quiet unassuming boy, who always did his work in a cheerful, willing manner. We miss him very much, and out sincerest sympathy is with you and your family in your great trouble'. (*Wakefield Express* 5 August 1916)

Mr and Mrs Earnshaw had last heard from Fred on 20 June 1916; after his death, Fred's friends Privates Dyson Lowrie and George Speight, who both worked with him at Charles Roberts', wrote that the last they saw of Fred was *'when he was leaping over the parapet; He was waving his rifle to them and was quite cheerful'.*

Company Sergeant Major Joseph Vaile
Prince of Wales Own (West Yorkshire) Regiment,
15th Battalion, Regimental Number 15/1272,
(Formerly 7681, 1st Grenadier Guards)

CSM Joseph Vaile also took part in the Battle of the Somme. Unlike many local men, however, Joseph had been a regular soldier.

Born in Gloucester in 1878, Joseph Vaile was the eldest of three boys born to George and Margaret Vaile.

Aged 18 years, Joseph left his work in a colliery and enlisted in Abertillary, Wales on the 27 May 1897 into the 3rd Battalion of the South Wales Borderers Regiment. His service number was 6381.

By 1901 Joseph had changed regiments and was now a private in the Grenadier Guards living in the Victoria Barracks in Windsor. He was 21 years of age. Fortunately, Joseph got through the Boer War (1889-1902) fighting in Soudan and South Africa without a scratch and was awarded the Queen's South Africa Medal.

Soon after discharge Joseph, aged 24, married 26 year old Henrietta Mason on 1 January 1902 in Morton near Bourne, Lincoln. By 1911 Joseph and Henrietta had four boys, seven-year old Joseph Leonard, five-year old William Henry, two-year old Francis Richard and five-month old Godfrey Sidney and were living in a four-roomed property in Wymondham, Oakham in Leicestershire. Joseph was working as a railway porter for the Midland Railway. At some stage in his railway career between 1911 and 1916, Joseph was promoted to signalman, and moved to live at New Scarborough in Netherton with his wife and sons.

When war came in 1914, as a Reservist from the Boer War, Joseph would have been called up and he was appointed Drill Instructor to the Leeds Pals.

The 15th Battalion, West Yorkshire Regiment (1st Leeds Pals) was raised in Leeds in September 1914 by the Lord Mayor and City. After training locally they moved to Silkstone in December 1914. In May 1915 the Battalion joined the 93rd Brigade, 31st Division and moved to South Camp, Ripon and later to Hurdcott Camp near Salisbury. In December 1915 they set sail for Alexandria in Egypt to defend the Suez Canal. In March 1916, the 31st Division left Port Said aboard HMT Briton bound for Marseilles in France, a journey which took 5 days. They travelled by train to Pont Remy, a few miles south east of Abbeville and marched to Bertrancourt arriving on 29 March 1916. Their first taste of action was at Serre on the Somme where they suffered heavy casualties as the battle was launched.

In the assault on the German lines on 1 July 1916, following an intense artillery bombardment, 31st Division (in which every Battalion was formed of 'Pals') was to attack and take the village of Serre. The 15th Battalion, advancing at 7.30am on 1 July, was decimated by German artillery and machine gun fire. Every officer

NETHERTON SERGEANT-MAJOR KILLED.

News has been received by Mrs. Vaile, New Scarboro', Netherton, of the death of her husband, Company Sergeant-Major Joseph Vaile, Grenadier Guards. The notice of the death was sent by Capt. A. Macdonald, which stated that the cause of death was wounds received in action on July 5th. Much sympathy is felt for Mrs. Vaile, who is left with six young boys, the eldest being only twelve years old. C.S.M. Vaile, who was a Welshman, was, prior to the outbreak of war, a signalman on the Midland Railway, and was a reservist, having gone through the Soudan and South African Wars without a scratch. On being called up at the beginning of the war he was appointed drill-instructor to the Leeds Pals, and in December last he was sent to Egypt, and in March came to France, and was home on leave only seven weeks ago.

Wakefield Express 15 July 1916

was killed or wounded, 233 other ranks were killed or died of wounds, 267 were wounded and 181 were missing. There were only 47 uninjured soldiers. The dead and wounded were brought in from No Man's Land for several days. Sergeant-Major Joseph Vaile died on 5 July 1916, from wounds sustained during the Battle of the Somme. He is buried in the St Pol Communal Cemetery Extension in France - Plot A24.

Henrietta Vaile remained a widow until her death aged 86 on 15 March 1962 in Headlands Hospital in Pontefract.

Private Gordon Land
King's Own Yorkshire Light Infantry
Regimental Number 200565

The first born and the only son of William Henry and Elizabeth Ann Land, Gordon was born 28 December 1896 in Thornhill Lees and baptised on 28 January 1897 in Thornhill Lees.

Gordon's father was a widower, his first wife, Margaret (nee Clarkson) having died, aged 31 years in the summer of 1890, leaving him with four children under the age of nine years, Arthur, Sarah, Edith and Florence.

Gordon was the fifth child of William's second marriage, to Elizabeth. In 1901 the family was living on Lees Hall Road in Thornhill Lees.

Gordon was educated at Ossett Grammar School and by 1911 was employed as a grocery assistant at the Cooperative Stores in Middlestown, along with several other young men who served in the army, including the Head Assistant, Wilfred Kaye.

When Great Britain declared war on Germany on the 4 August 1914, Gordon would have have been only 17 years old. Soon after his 18th birthday in 1915, he enlisted with theh the King's Own Yorkshire Light Infantry (KOYLI) at Dewsbury.

Wakefield Express 29 July 1916

Gordon was killed taking part in the Battle of the Somme. Initially missing, it was some some time before his death was confirmed and his body was never found.

The War Diary for 1/4 KOYLI records that on the 6 July 1916:

W and Z Companies were employed carrying bombs and ammunition to "A" Line. We later received orders to take over "A" Line from 5th KOYLI. Major H. Moorhouse, DSO was put in charge of the Sector.

7:15pm: Two parties of bombers under 2nd Lt. E.E. Greenhough and 2nd Lt. D.C. Moodie respectively volunteered to advance up the trenches leading to the German lines at A.19 and B.19 respectively from A.17 with a view to extending our line and pushing back the hostile bombers. These parties advanced and succeeded in establishing blocks 70 yards in advance of positions previously held by us.

Capt. H.G. Fraser and 2nd Lt. F.G. Kaye arrived to replace casualties."

It is possible that Private Land was killed as a part of one of these two raiding parties, but it is more likely that he was killed shortly after midnight into the 7 July 1916 when the 1/4 KOYLI War Diary tells us of a major German attack on the KOYLI positions resulting in many deaths:

On the 7 July 1916, the 1/4 Battalion, KOYLI were in the Thiepval sector during the Battle of the Somme, taking part in an attack on the village of 'Ovillers' (North of Thiepval on the Albert-Bapaume Road). Their "War Diary" for the 7 July 1916 records the following:

"12:30 a.m. - Enemy opened intense bombardment on original British front line. This continued until 2:15 a.m., our artillery replying effectively."

"02:15 a.m. - The bombardment was turned on to the 'A' Line until 02:50 a.m. when it was turned again on to the communications trenches and lines behind."

"02:50 a.m. - Enemy bombers advanced down the trench towards A.18 and A.16 and across the open to A.17, a furious fight with bombs ensued lasting until 06:30 a.m. Numerous casualties were incurred both from bombs, and enemy snipers who were lying out in the open and who shot down our men as they fired and threw bombs out of the trench. Major H. Moorhouse, D.S.O. in command of the sector was wounded in the arm by a sniper about 04:00 a.m., but remained in command until 05:30 a.m. when forced through loss of blood to go to the Dressing Station, Captain W. M. Williamson, commanding 'Z' Company, and 2/Lts. Carter, Massie, Mackay, De Jonquet and Huntington were also wounded. Capt. H.G. Fraser took command and continued the fight until 06:30 a.m. when he ran out of bombs and was forced to retire down the communications trench to the original British Front Line which he held along with the 4th and 5th Y. & L. Regiment already there with the 35 men remaining out of the two companies until 09:30 a.m. when he was ordered to return to the Assembly Trenches in Thiepval Wood."

"Casualties: Other Ranks, 20 killed and 180 wounded."

Private Bernard Howden
Duke of Wellington's West Riding Regiment
1/4 Battn
Service no 202776

Bernard and Herbert Howden were the sons of Elizabeth and Alfred Howden of Middlestown. Their father was a miner.

For a few years around 1891 the family lived in West Ardsley and Bernard was born there. By 1901, however, their mother had been widowed and the family, which by then comprised Herbert and Bernard together with their sisters Ethel and Doris, were living on Thornhill Road, Middlestown and Herbert, aged 13 years, was working as a rope ender in the pit.

By 1911 their mother had remarried; their stepfather was Robert Brooke, also from Middlestown, who was employed in the colliery as a Banksman. At this time Bernard was a miner. They, with their parents, two sisters and Robert Brooke's granddaughter were living in a house with four rooms in Middlestown.

Bernard became a regular soldier in the Duke of Wellington's West Riding Regiment. He and his brother were among those who received cards letters and parcels 'for our gallant defenders' at Christmas 1914.

The Territorial 1/4 Battalion had been formed in Halifax in August 1914 as a part of the 2nd West Riding Brigade, West Riding Division. They moved on mobilisation to coastal defences near Hull and Grimsby and moved again on the 5 November 1914 to billets in Doncaster. On the 14 April 1915 the battalion landed at Boulogne and on 15 May 1915 the formation became 147th Brigade in 49th (West Riding) Division.

Between 23 July and 3 September 1916, the battalion as part of 49th (West Riding) Division were engaged in the Battle of Pozières Ridge. Private Howden was killed on the last day of the battle on the 3 September 1916.

In the north of the Somme battlefield, comparatively little progress had been made. Thiepval, which stood on a prominent ridge, had been surrounded on three sides by the end of August, but was still holding out. It had become an annoying salient jutting into the British lines. By holding onto the village, the Germans were able to prevent the British from occupying the whole of the ridge from Thiepval down to Pozières.

A renewed attempt to take Thiepval was planned for 3 September; this attack was to take place using three divisions, one of which was to be the 49th (West Riding) Division.

The 49th Division was to have two brigades making the attack: 146 Brigade on the left and 147 Brigade on the right. 146 Brigade had the 1/8th West Yorkshire Regiment on the left of the assault and the 1/6th West Yorkshires on the right. 147 Brigade attacked with the 1/5th Duke of Wellington's Regiment on the left, and the 1/4th Duke of Wellington's on the right.

The war diary of the 1/5th Duke of Wellington's Regiment describes in two sentences the result of the attack:

> The whole attack failed. The 146 Brigade did not reach its objective and although the 147 Brigade reached their objective, they were unable to hold it.

Private Bernard Howden was doubtless killed in this failed engagement and his body was never found. He is remembered on Pier and Face 6 A and 6 B of the Thiepval Memorial, the monument to the missing on which 72,000 names are recorded.

Rifleman James Henry Proctor
King's Royal Rifle Corps
9th Battalion/21Bttn
R/9806

James Henry Proctor was born in Birmingham on 2 June 1893 to James Henry and Sarah Proctor. His father was a Prison Officer and was employed as a tailor instructor. His children were born in Walton, Liverpool, Durham and Wakefield, indicating perhaps his moves to different prisons around the country.

By 1911 the family was living in Lincoln Street Wakefield and James Henry Proctor, aged 17 years old, was a pupil teacher at an elementary school; from 1911 to 1912 he was a pupil teacher at Netherton School.

From 1907 to 1911 Henry James Proctor had been a pupil at Wakefield Grammar School and when he enlisted in York in the King's Royal Rifle Corps on 29 November 1915 he was a Student at St John's College, York.

The 21st (Service) Battalion (Yeoman Rifles) was formed in September 1915 from volunteers from the farming communities of Yorkshire, Northumberland and Durham by the Northern Command. They moved to Duncombe Park at Helmsley, the seat of the Earl of Faversham, colonel of the regiment, in January 1916 and came under orders of 124th Brigade in 41st Division. On the 4th May 1916, the Battalion landed in France.

Two months before he had enlisted he the 'former assistant' visited the school. He was obviously fondly remembered both in Netherton and at Wakefield Grammar School.

Rifleman James Henry Proctor was killed in action in France on 15 September 1916 at Flers at the Battle of Flers-Courcelette, which lasted from the 15 to 22 September and saw tanks employed for the first time in history. These primitive tanks came from C Company and D Company of the Machine Gun Corps.

"The 41st Division was to attack Flers and had most tanks, four for the Longueval–Flers road and six to attack the middle and west side of the village. On the right flank the 124th Brigade attacked with two battalions forward and two in support, having assembled in no man's land. The advance began at zero hour and Tea Support Trench and the Switch Line fell relatively easily by 7:00 a.m. and Flers Trench at 7:50 a.m. At 3:20 p.m. a large party of infantry reached Bulls Road and linked with the 122nd Brigade on the left, but attacks on Gird Trench failed."

Here is the War Diary extract for the 21st Battalion, K.R.R.C. for September 15th, 16th and 17th, 1916:

DELVILLE WOOD: September 15th 1916

The Battalion took part in an attack on the enemy lines in front of DELVILLE WOOD. The 124th Brigade advanced on a line which passed between the villages of FLERS on the left and GUEUDECOURT on the right. The Battalion was on the left of the first line with the 10th Queens on the right and the 26th and 32nd Royal Fusiliers in support. The 122nd Brigade was on the left and the 14th Division on the right. The attack started at 6.30 after artillery and the first objective the SWITCH

TRENCH was taken without difficulty practically no living enemy being encountered. After further artillery preparation the attacking force went on and took the second objective the FLERS TRENCH where a few prisoners were taken, but the enemy showed little disposition to fight. During this stage of the advance the Battalion suffered rather heavily through getting too near our own barrage. It was found impossible to continue the advance, owing to lack of support on the flanks and the line of the second objective was consolidated.

During this stage of the operations the Battalion lost 2nd Lts. Hervey, Benton and Nivison killed. Capts Watson Pitt, Law and Coates, and 2nd Lts. Waldy, Yeaman and Jones wounded.

Late in the day Lt. Col the Earl of Feversham went forward with Lt. Col Oakley of the 10th Queens and as many men as could be collected to the third and fourth objectives in front of GUEUDECOURT village. They reached the third objective and successfully withstood more than one counter attack. During this time Lt Col the Earl of Feversham was killed. They were eventually forced to retire and consolidate on a line about 400 yards in front of the second objective when the remnants of the Battalion remained until relieved at about 3 a.m. Killed: 4 officers and 54 Other Ranks, Wounded: 10 officers and 256 Other Ranks

Missing: 70 Other Ranks (Including Rifleman James Henry Proctor)

The following obituary appeared in the Wakefield Grammar School's Old Savilians' Commemorative number:

Jim Proctor can be remembered by many of us now at school. He was a loyal and devoted soul and was never happier than when doing something for the credit of the place he loved so well. "Deeds rather than words" was always his motto, and such Old Savilians are of very great value in these troublous times…

The Netherton School log book records on 4 October 1916 that 'The Headmaster received the painful news this morning announcing the death of Mr James Henry Proctor, former assistant master at the school. He was killed in action between 15th and 17th of September'.

Kirkgate Station.

ANOTHER OLD WAKEFIELD GRAMMAR SCHOOL BOY KILLED.

HIGHLY THOUGHT OF BY HIS OFFICERS AND COMRADES.

Official news has been received of the death in action of Rifleman James Henry Proctor, son of Mr. J. H. Proctor, Plumpton-road, Westgate, Wakefield, which took place on Sept. 15th whilst he was serving with the King's Royal Rifle Corps. A letter was received on Wednesday morning from the Wesleyan Chaplain, attached to the Brigade, as follows :—

" As you probably know your son's battalion took part in a very important and successful attack nearly a fortnight ago. I have delayed writing to you until now in hope that some less serious word could be sent, but the battalion headquarters staff give me no ground for such hope now. Your brave son is reported as killed in action on Sept. 15th. He was very highly thought of by his officers and comrades. I was always glad when I could have a chat with him in the trenches or at the billets and when he was able to be at our services. We all join to think of your great sorrow with all respect and sympathy. As soon as possible I held service and communion for our men on the Friday after the engagement, and both then and on the following Sunday we stood at the salute for a few moments in honour of those who had been "faithful unto death," and we earnestly remembered all at home who will be sorrowing for them. I hope you will be able to think of your boy not as having 'lost' his life but as having 'gained' it most truly in giving it for us all in such a spirit."

Rifleman Proctor was educated at the Wakefield Grammar School and St. John's College, York, where he was a student at the time of his enlistment last year in the battalion raised by the late Earl Feversham, who was killed in action on the same day. Any news as to the manner of his death from his late soldier chums will be greatly welcomed by his parents.

Wakefield Express 7 October 1916

The school war memorial was unveiled at a ceremony attended by his mother and brother and is inscribed.

Rifleman Proctor's body was never found and he is remembered on panels 13a/13B of the Memorial to the Missing at Thiepval.

Rifleman Edward Earnshaw
King's Royal Rifle Corps,
21st Battallion
Regimental Number R/19476

Edward Earnshaw was killed on the same day and in the same action as Rifleman James Henry Proctor and is commemorated on the same panel of the Thiepval Memorial.

Edward was the sixth and youngest child born to Ben and Mary Hannah Earnshaw. He was affectionately known as Teddie by the family.

Edward spent his childhood in Midgley and his family home was one of The Limes, a pair of semi-detached houses built by Ben and William Earnshaw in 1884 in the field above the wood yard where they worked.

The Limes

Edward is remembered on the war memorial in St Andrew's Church, Netherton, the memorial at Midgley and on the family grave stone in Thornhill Churchyard. His body was never found and, like that of Rifleman Proctor, his name is inscribed on panels 13A/13B on the memorial for the Missing at Thiepval, France.

Private Walter Earnshaw
Duke of Wellington's Regiment (West Riding)
1/4 Battalion
Regimental Number 203291

Walter Earnshaw was the son of William Earnshaw and his wife, Martha (nee Townsend). He was born in Midgley on 12 August 1888 when his father, William, was 39 and his mother, Martha was 41. He was the youngest in the family with six brothers and two sisters. They lived in one of The Limes, next door to the family of Teddie Earnshaw described above. Walter was educated at Wakefield Grammar School and subsequently worked as a clerk at the Earnshaw family timber yard.

Walter enlisted in the Duke of Wellington's West Riding Regiment at Huddersfield on 10 April 1915 and embarked for France and Flanders around 25 August 1916.

1/4 Duke of Wellington's Regiment was one of the regiment's three Territorial battalions (the other two were 5th and 6th), based in Halifax, Yorkshire, part of the 2nd West Riding Brigade (later 147th), West Riding Division (later 49th).

For the first three months of the war it was on coast defence near Hull and Grimsby before moving to Doncaster, where it remained until embarking for France on 14 April 1915, landing in Boulogne. The battalion fought on the Western Front for the rest of the war, staying in the same brigade and division. The formation became 147th Brigade in 49th (West Riding) Division on the 15 May 1915.

Walter Earnshaw was reported missing after the fighting at Delville Wood during the Battle of the Somme and declared killed in action on Sunday 17 September 1916, the same day as his cousin Edward.

Walter was awarded the British and Victory medals for his service in WW1 and, like his nephew Fred Earnshaw, Rifleman Proctor and many more, he is remembered at the Thiepval Memorial, in northern France, Pier & Face 6a & 6b.

The register of Soldier's Effects shows that Walter's mother was the sole legatee of his cash - £6.12s.22d.

Acting Sergeant Thomas Saunders
10th KOYLI
18610

Thomas was born in Liverpool, the son of Thomas and Alice Saunders, of 91, Wordsworth St., Hartington Rd., Liverpool. His father Thomas was a seaman and he had been lost at sea; two of his brothers served at sea.

At the time of the 1911 census, a Thomas Saunders, then an apprentice painter aged 17, and his widowed mother, Mary Alice Saunders, were boarding with another seafaring family, Thomas Toner and his wife Kate, at no 1, Greyrock Street, West Derby Road [Liverpool].

At some point, Thomas Saunders moved to Overton, where he lodged with the family of Friend Taylor, whose son Willie died at Gallipoli.

Thomas worked at Wood Pit, Denby Grange Collieries and was a member of the Denby Grange Collieries Cricket Club and Middlestown Athletic Club.

At the beginning of the war, Thomas enlisted in Dewsbury in the 10th (Service) Battalion of the King's Own Yorkshire Light Infantry.

The 10th (Service) Battalion, KOYLI was formed at Pontefract in September 1914 as part of K3 and came under command of 64th Brigade in 21st Division. They moved to Berkhamsted and then to Halton Park (Tring) in October 1914, going on to billets in Maidenhead in November. They returned to Halton Park in April 1915 and went on to Witley in August. In September 1915, the battalion landed in France.

On the 16 September 1916, 64th Brigade was attached to 41st Division and they were involved in an attack on Gird Trench (between Flers and Gueudecourt). 64th Brigade formed the main attack and they experienced great difficulty in coming up to the front position in the darkness and rain. 15th Durham Light Infantry and 9th KOYLI were in front, with 10th KOYLI and the 1st East Yorkshires in support. They advanced some 1,300 yards behind the British artillery barrage, which was weak and inaccurate, but were late in starting. As a consequence, they suffered considerably from machine gun fire and shrapnel before reaching the existing forward positions. A few troops got within 100 yards of Gird Trench, but could not push the attack home. A tank (D14) overtook the KOYLI troops and went on to Guadecourt, but was hit by a shell and wrecked. 64th Brigade rallied at Bulls Road, but an order for the renewal of the attack came too late in the evening to be acted upon.

On the 17 September 1916, 10th KOYLI were in defensive positions in Flers Trench in the build up to the Battle of Morval. The *Wakefield*

A MIDDLESTOWN SOLDIER KILLED.

News was received on Monday morning that Sergt. Thomas Saunders (K.O.Y.L.I.) was killed in the trenches on September 17th, death being instantaneous. Deceased was 23 years of age, and prior to joining the colours at the beginning of the war he worked at Wood Pit, Denby Grange Collieries. He belonged to a fighting family. He has two brothers serving as sailors, and his father, who was also a sailor, was drowned at sea. Before enlisting he lived for a number of years with Mr. and Mrs. Friend Taylor, of Overton. He was a member of the Middlestown Athletic Club and also a member of the Denby Grange Collieries Cricket Club. Letters from comrades spoke highly of the qualities of Saunders, and when he received two stripes he was known as "the prowling corporal."

Wakefield Express 21 October 1916 p9

Express of 21 October 1916 records that Sergeant Thomas Saunders was killed instantaneously on that day; his body was not recovered and his name, like those of Fred and Walter Earnshaw and James Henry Proctor, is recorded on the monument to the missing at Thiepval. He was 23 years old. His effects were left to his mother Alice.

1917

Driver Herbert Howden
Royal Field Artillery C battery 71st Brigade
26100

Herbert Howden (Holden) was the son of Elizabeth and Alfred Howden of Middlestown and the brother of Bernard, whose story appears above. Herbert was baptised at St Luke's Church, Middlestown, on 15 February 1888 and by 1901, after leaving school, Herbert was working in the pit as a rope ender.

By 1911 his widowed mother had remarried; Herbert's stepfather was Robert Brooke, also from Middlestown, a Banksman in the colliery. At that time Herbert was a blacksmith and his brother Bernard a miner.

Herbert enlisted as a Driver in the army in 1914. He and his brother both received cards letters and parcels 'for our gallant defenders' at Christmas 1914.

In April 1917, Herbert was reported to have been severely wounded during the First Battle of the Scarpe, fought between the 9 and 14 April 1917. The Battle of the Scarpe (named after the River Scarpe which runs through the centre of the battlefield) was part of the larger Battle of Arras.

MIDDLESTOWN SOLDIER SEVERELY WOUNDED.

News has this week been received that Driver Herbert Holden, eldest son of Mr. and Mrs. Robert Brooke, Church Terrace, Middlestown, has been severely wounded. The unfortunate young man joined up at the beginning of the war, and was drafted out to France at once. He was over on leave about 12 months ago, suffering from shell shock. His younger brother, Pte. Bernard Holden, who was in the Regular Army, was reported missing last July, and although continued inquiries have been made by his parents and friends, nothing further has been heard from him. The nature of Driver Holden's wounds is not yet known.

Wakefield Express 21 April 1917 p6

Driver Herbert Howden, aged 29 years, son of Mrs. Elizabeth Brooke, of 4, Belmont Terrace, Middlestown, died on the 10 April 1917 and is buried in Duisans British Cemetery, Etrun.

Sadly, in the six months from September 1916 to April 1917, twice widowed Elizabeth Brooke had lost both her sons, a devastating reflection of the effect of war on so many local families.

George Schofield Glover
58th Infantry Battalion
Australian Army
Regimental Number 2173

George, and probably his brother Thomas, were educated at St Peter's School in Horbury. Aged 15 years or thereabouts, George left school and went to work as a clerk in the offices of Charles Roberts & Co. at Horbury Junction (the same firm at which Fred Earnshaw and several other local soldiers were employed).

After being there about a year, however, George left to work as a railway clerk at Walton, where he stayed for four years.

By 1911, George is shown on the Census Returns as being a serving soldier in the Pontefract barracks, aged 20 years. He later served in Singapore.

At the age of 24 years he took discharge from the Army and moved to Australia, where he once more worked as a clerk.

George was living at 155, Flemington Road in North Melbourne, Victoria Australia as a single man when he enlisted on 11 March 1915. He embarked from Melbourne on the 17 June 1915 on the HMAT Wandilla A62, a steamship built in 1912

for the Adelaide Steamship Company. The ship operated on the Fremantle to Sydney run until 1915, when she was acquired for military service and re-designated HMAT Wandilla. Initially used as a troop transport, the vessel was converted to a hospital ship in 1916. Wandilla was returned to her owners at the end of the war.

The photograph below shows the diggers of the 3rd Pioneer Battalion preparing to board HMAT Wandilla at Port Melbourne, bound for the Western Front on the 6 June 1916.

Possibly due to his earlier experience as a soldier, George was soon promoted to Sergeant and served in the 58th Battalion.

The 58th Battalion drew its experienced personnel from the 6th Battalion while its new recruits came from Victoria. Together with

the 57th, 59th and 60th Battalions, the 58th formed part of the 15th Brigade, which was attached to the 5th Australian Division. At this time it was decided that the Australian infantry divisions would be transferred to Europe to fight in the trenches along the Western Front in France and Belgium. As the 5th Division was still forming it did not depart until later in the year and the 58th Battalion arrived in France on 23 June 1916.

The battalion experienced its first taste of fighting on the Western Front in July 1916 when it was involved in the Battle of Fromelles, being in reserve and providing medical stretcher parties.

During early 1917, in an effort to shorten their lines of communication, the Germans withdrew to prepared positions of the Hindenburg Line; a brief advance followed as the Allies followed them up. During this phase of the war the 58th Battalion was not committed to any major attacks, but it did play a defensive role at the end of the Second Battle of Bullecourt in May, holding the ground that the Australians had gained earlier.

The Second Battle of Bullecourt began at 3.45 a.m. on the 3 May 1917 with eight successive waves of infantry, this time supported by artillery fire. The Australians broke through the partially destroyed barbed wire entanglements, passing many of their comrades killed the month before and still lying in the mud.

The 5th Brigade, cut to pieces by machine gun fire, was forced to withdraw before crossing the barbed wire and this brought to a halt the following waves of infantry. A few young officers intervened to get the men moving forward again but by the end of the day no real gain had been made and the Second Battle of Bullecourt deteriorated into a tragic repetition of the first. Only the survivors of the 6th Brigade managed to take 400 metres of the German Front and press on to the second line, receiving reinforcements under cover of night.

In the following days the Australians strengthened their positions and dug a communication trench back to their home line to collect fresh munitions and evacuate the wounded. Despite a German counter-attack on 6 May, the British 7th Division gained a foothold in the ruins of Bullecourt on 7 May and subsequently connected with the Australian bridgehead. In the following days the British and Australians were subjected to continuous shelling and, in some areas, the Germans attacked with flame-throwers. Sporadic fighting broke out over the next few days but all action ceased on 15 May.

The Second Battle of Bullecourt inflicted 7,000 more losses on the Australians with very little to show for the effort except for the capture of a minute portion of the Hindenburg Line. The Australian troops had been pushed to the extreme and exhibited some defiance towards the British command.

Sergeant George Schofield Glover, aged 27 years, died of wounds on the 14 May 1917 during fighting in the 2nd Battle of Bullecourt and is buried in the Grevillers British Cemetery, Picardie, France at Plot V, Row A, Grave No. 1.

Upon enlistment, George had given his mother as next of kin - Mrs Martha Mountain of Ivy Cottage, Netherton, Yorkshire, a house adjacent to St Andrew's Church. George's mother Martha had married Tom Mountain in St Luke's Church Middlestown on 6 April 1896.

George is remembered on the war memorial in St Andrew's Church and upon his grandparent's grave in Horbury Cemetery. From the family gravestone in Horbury Cemetery, it is evident that his Uncle Harry also lost his life in the First World War.

Sadly George's brother Thomas Henry Glover died aged 25 years in 1920 from sickness following gas poisoning in the First World War and is buried in Horbury cemetery. He had served as a private in the 4th Reserve Garrison Battalion of KOYLI - Regimental Number 20165.

Private R. John Schooling
Army Cyclist Corps, 11th Cyclist Battalion 8763
formerly West Yorkshire Regiment

John Schooling, the son of Albert and Sophia Schooling, was born in Peckham in about 1896.

He lived with Mr and Mrs Isaac Parrott of Wichentree Hall, Sandy Lane, Middlestown and worked at Caphouse Pit, Denby Grange Colliery.

He enlisted in Leeds in December 1914 and was attached to the Army Cyclist Corps.

The primary roles of the cyclists were reconnaissance and communications (message taking). They were armed as infantry and could provide mobile firepower if required. Those units that went overseas continued in these roles but also (once the mobile phase of war had settled down into entrenched warfare) spent much time in trench-holding duties and on manual work.

Cyclists were used by the British, German, French and Belgian armies and in fact the first British soldier to be killed in Western Europe in 1914 was a cyclist. (He and a colleague were acting as scouts riding ahead of the infantry when they bumped into a group of German Jägers).

The 11th Corps Cyclist Battalion appears to have been formed on 10 May 1916 from the Divisional Cyclist companies of the 33rd, 35th (Bantam) and 38th (Welsh) Divisions. 33rd Div Cy Coy was probably formed at Clipstone Camp, 35th Div Cy Coy on Salisbury Plain and 38th Div Cy Coy at Conway, all during the divisional assembly periods in 1915.

hands, and has all that skill and care can provide."

Mr. and Mrs. Isaac Parrott, Wichentree Hall, Middlestown, have this week received information that Private John A. E. Schooling has died from wounds. Schooling, who resided with Mr. and Mrs. Parrott, enlisted in December, 1914, and was at Middlestown on leave on Nov. 3rd, 1915, going to France in January, 1916. Before enlisting he worked at Caphouse Pit, Denby Grange Collieries. A letter from deceased's company commander says: — "Schooling was an excellent soldier and a fine sportsman, and liked by everyone. He died as the result of wounds caused by shell fire. The funeral takes place to-day (May 11th), and he will be buried with full military honours."

Mrs. Brunt, Montagu-street, Sandal.

Wakefield Express 19 May 1917

11th Corps went to Italy in November 1917, returning to the Western Front in March 1918. It is not clear where Private Schooling was wounded by shell fire; it is probable that he died in the Military Hospital at Merville where he was subsequently buried in grave number 111.A.19 in the MERVILLE COMMUNAL CEMETERY EXTENSION, which was opened in August 1916, and used by Commonwealth and Portuguese hospitals until April 1918.

Pte Schooling's effects of £53:11s:11d were left to Lettice (Lettie) Kellett, to whom probate was granted.

Private Robert Edwin Stubbs
Coldstream Guards
3rd Battalion
19455

Robert Edwin Stubbs was the son of Thomas Edwin and Fanny Stubbs of Blackpool, previously of Ossett.

He was baptised on 2 December 1894 in Horbury; at that time his father was described as an artist.

In 1901 the family were living in Albert Street, Ossett and they were still there in 1911, by which time sixteen year old Robert Edwin was employed by Ossett Co-op as a butcher.

On 15 February 1915, twenty year old Robert Edwin married nineteen year old Sarah Lydia Metcalfe in St Luke's Church, Middlestown. Sarah's father, Frederick, was a blacksmith and Thomas Edwin Stubbs was an artist.

Edwin Stubbs enlisted in the 3rd Battalion Coldstream Guards, which was part of the 1st Guards Brigade in 1917.

The Guards Division spent the winter of 1916/17 holding the front line on the Somme, but did not fight at Arras in 1917. Instead they moved up to the Ypres Salient and took over the Canal Sector at Boesinghe. During Third Ypres they fought in the Battle of Pilckem Ridge from 31 July - 2 August when they captured the German positions around Artillery Wood, and returned to Flanders for the Battle of Poelcapelle and Passchendaele in October 1917.

It is likely that Private Stubbs was wounded during the Battle of Pilckem Ridge between the 31 July 1917 and 3 August 1917 and was taken to the military

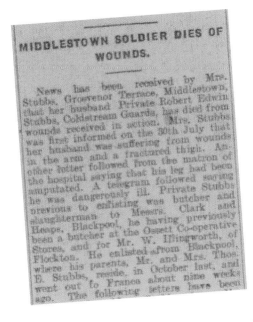

MIDDLESTOWN SOLDIER DIES OF WOUNDS.

News has been received by Mrs. Stubbs, Grosvenor Terrace, Middlestown, that her husband Private Robert Edwin Stubbs, Coldstream Guards, has died from wounds received in action. Mrs. Stubbs was first informed on the 30th July that her husband was suffering from wounds in the arm and a fractured thigh. Another letter followed from the matron of the hospital saying that his leg had been amputated. A telegram followed saying he was dangerously ill. Private Stubbs previous to enlisting was butcher and slaughterman to Messrs. Clark and Heaps, Blackpool, he having previously been a butcher at the Ossett Co-operative Stores, and for Mr. W. Illingworth, of Flockton. He enlisted from Blackpool, where his parents, Mr. and Mrs. Thos. E. Stubbs, reside, in October last, and went out to France about nine weeks ago. The following letters have been

ago. The following letters have been received by Mrs. Stubbs from Mr. J. W. J. Bennett, Church of England Chaplain:—"August 11th, 1917. Dear Mrs. Stubbs.—You will have heard that your husband has passed away. He bore his pain and suffering most bravely, like a true soldier. I was able to be with him in his last moments, and he was quite content to go to his Saviour." In another letter received on Thursday morning by Mrs. Metcalfe, mother-in-law, Mr. Bennett says he administered the Holy Communion to him on the morning that he died. He was perfectly conscious, and received the sacrament with great devotion. "He bore his sufferings bravely and patiently, like a good soldier of Jesus Christ, and you may feel proud of being the mother of so brave and good a lad." The Chaplain added: "In beautiful sunshine and under a clear blue sky, his coffin, covered with white flowers, was laid in the grave."

Wakefield Express 18 August 1917

hospital at Wimereux, Pas de Calais, where he died from wounds on the 10 August 1917.

From October 1914 onwards, Boulogne and Wimereux formed an important hospital centre and until June 1918, the medical units at Wimereux used the communal cemetery for burials, the south-eastern half having been set aside for Commonwealth graves, although a few burials were also made among the civilian graves.

Sarah Lydia Stubbs remarried on 21 September 1919, in Blackpool. She had been a widow since 1917 and was still only 24 years old. Her new husband was William Spencer Miller, 26, a plumber.

Bugler Sydney Lockwood
6th Battalion
KOYLI

Sydney was brought up in Alpha House, Whinney Lane, Streethouse. In 1901 his father, George H. Lockwood, was a forty-two year old miner, working as a hewer. George was born in Huddersfield and his wife Ruth Ann was from Honley.

By 1911, Father had died and there was only sixteen-year old Sydney and thirteen-year old Florrie at home. Sydney was working as a colliery driver below ground and the family lived at 18, Milton Street, Streethouse with their fifty-four year old mother, Ruth.

Sydney enlisted in the King's Own Yorkshire Infantry in Leeds.

The 6th (Service) Battalion, Kings Own Yorkshire Light Infantry was raised at Pontefract on the 12 August 1914 as part of Kitchener's First New Army and joined 43rd Brigade in 14th (Light) Division. They trained at Woking, moving to Witley in November 1914 for the winter, and then moving to Aldershot in February 1915 for final training. They proceeded to France on the 21 May 1915 landing at Boulogne. They fought in the Action of Hooge, being the first division to be attacked by flamethrowers. They were in action in The Second Attack on Bellewaarde. In 1916 they were on the Somme seeing action in The Battle of Delville Wood and The Battle of Flers-Courcelette.

In 1917 they fought in the German retreat to the Hindenburg Line, The First and Third Battle of the Scarpe at Arras, The Battle of Langemark and The First and Second Battle of Passchendaele. On the 19 February 1918 the 6th KOYLI were disbanded in France as the army was reorganised.

Bugler Sydney Lockwood died on the 22 August 1917 in action with 6th KOYLI

Langemarck Memorial

in 43 Brigade, 14th (Light) Division during a follow-up action after the Battle of Langemarck, 16 to 18 August 1917 as part of the 3rd Battle of Ypres in Belgium.

During the afternoon of the 22 August 1917 concentrations of the enemy were dispersed by artillery fire and an attack on the right was beaten off by small arms fire. However, three companies of the 6th Bn. KOYLI had now become involved in the fight, so the 8th Bn. 60th (41st Brigade) was ordered to relieve one company of the 6th KOYLI in the original front line of the 43rd Brigade.

Sydney Lockwood died of wounds on that day. He is buried in Bedford House Cemetery, Ypres, West Flanders, Belgium and is commemorated in Trinity Methodist Church, Netherton. His brothers and sisters received his effects.

Private Leonard Shires
1st/4th
KOYLI 6th Battalion
200780

The son of Squire Shires and his wife Ann (nee Walshaw), Leonard was born in Overton on 16 January 1894 and baptised in Horbury on 6 March 1894. His mother died when Leonard was barely one year old and his father married again on 11 September 1899.

Leonard was adopted by his uncle and aunt, Benjamin and Mary Gawthorpe, who brought him up as their son. The family lived at Stoneycliffe Cottages, Middlestown in 1901, but later moved to Church Villas, Middlestown.

Before enlisting, Leonard had worked as a blacksmith at Denby Grange Collieries. He was a Sunday School teacher at St Luke's Church and a member of the choir, as well as being a member of Denby Grange Colliery Cricket Club and of Middlestown Institute.

Leonard had been in France for only about twelve weeks when he was killed, aged twenty-three years at Inverness Copse during a follow up operation on the 24 August 1917 at the Battle of Langemarck in Belgium. On 22 August, the 14th (Light) Division, including 6 KOYLI, as part of 43 Brigade, captured Inverness

IN **MIDDLESTOWN SOLDIER KILLED.**

News was received yesterday week that Private Leonard Shires, of Middlestown, had been killed in action in France. Mr. and Mrs. Benjamin Goldthorpe, with whom deceased lived, received a letter from Second-Lieutenant G. G. Stephenson, who stated that Shires was killed on August 23rd. The officer added: "He will be greatly missed by me and everyone in the platoon, as his sterling qualities were recognised by all with whom he came in contact. He was everything that could be desired, he was brave and devoted to his duty, and died like a hero." Pte. Shires was brought up from childhood by Mr. and Mrs. Goldthorpe, and prior to enlisting on October 28th, 1914, he worked as a blacksmith at the Denby Grange Collieries. He had been in France only about twelve weeks. He was a Sunday School teacher at St. Luke's and a member of the choir. He was also a prominent member of the Denby Grange Colliery Cricket Club, and also of the Middlestown Institute. He was 23 years of age.

Langemarck

Wakefield Express
8 September 1917

Tyne Cot

Tyne Cot

Copse and then lost it to a German methodical counter-attack (Gegenangriff) on the 24 August when Private Shires lost his life.

Private Shires is commemorated on the Tyne Cot Memorial and in St Luke's Church, Overton.

Signaller Wilfred Kaye
1st/4th
KOYLI
203172

Also commemorated at Tyne Cot is Signaller Wilfred Kaye. Wilfred was the son of Wilson Morley Kaye and his wife Elizabeth Anne. Wilfred was born in the parish of Kirkburton on 5 May 1889 and baptised in Shelley on 10 August 1902 along with his sister Nellie, although by then they were living in Church Terrace, Middlestown. By 1911 Wilfred's father was the caretaker for St Luke's Church and School and the family was living in St Luke's Cottage.

Before enlisting with several of his work colleagues, Wilfred was employed at Middlestown Co-operative Stores as the Head Assistant.

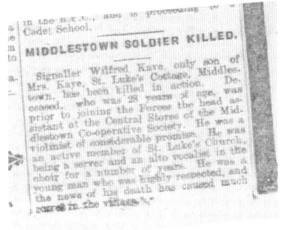

Wakefield Express 27 October 1917

A gifted musician, Wilfred played the violin in a string quartet which provided entertainment at many local events. He was an active member of St Luke's Church, for which his father was the caretaker, acting as a Server and singing in the choir.

'A young man who was highly respected', Signaller Wilfred Kaye died on the 9 October 1917 during the intense fighting of the Battle of Poelkapelle part of the Third Battle for Ypres, in Belgium and known as Passchendaele.

Signaller Wilfred Kaye's 148th Brigade in the 49th Division took part in II Anzac Corps' attack at Poelcapelle on the 9th October 1917.

Zero hour on 9 October 1917 was 05:20am, when the British Artillery barrage came down promptly on the enemy's front line and his emplacements. But the ground was sodden, inches deep in mud and in an altogether appalling condition, so that many H.E. shells did not explode. The heavy rain of the previous day and night had turned No Man's Land into a veritable quagmire.

The 49th Division, 148th Brigade advance that day comprised 1/4 (Hallamshire) York and Lancasters on the right hand side of the Grafenstafel road (Bellvue Spur, Ravebeek area) and the 1/5 King's Own Yorkshire Light Infantry to their left (left hand side of the road) with 1/7 Battalion West Yorks further to their left and the 1/5 York and Lancasters to the rear (Fleet Cottage area.)

The 148th Brigade on the right of the 49th Division advance, stalled in the swamp astride the Ravebeek and only a few parties managed to get across the water which was now some 30 to 50 yards wide and waist deep at its midpoint. The creeping barrage was thin and moved at 100 yards in six minutes, which proved too fast for the infantry. The 1/4 KOYLI, previously in reserve was sent up to reinforce the attack. The whole Brigade was now in one line. They advanced up a long slope and came under fire from Wolf Copse on the left and Bellevue on the top of the slope. Casualties forced the troops to dig in along the slope. At 7 pm, an attempt was made to take the two pillboxes on the ridge but they were so heavily wired that the attack had to be abandoned.

The enemy were identified as the 5th Jäger Regiment who were able to fire through the artillery barrage. By the afternoon of the 9 October 1917, the 148th and 146th Brigades were near the red line, having suffered 2,500 casualties. 148 Brigade was relieved by the NZ Battalions at 10.30pm on the 10th October. Eventually the reserves were brought up to consolidate the first objective and to 'dig in' in front of the German wire. The casualties of the division in this attack were 2,585 of which 654, including Wilfred Kaye, were fatalities.

Wilfred Kaye has no known grave, but he is remembered on the memorial at Tyne Cot, on his parents' grave in Kirkburton Churchyard, on the war memorial in St Luke's Church, Overton and in the stained glass window depicting St Wilfred, commissioned by his mother and sisters and dedicated in 1920.

Corporal Edgar Sutcliffe
10th Battalion
KOYLI
19061

Edgar Sutcliffe was the son of John and Mary Sutcliffe of Thornhill. Edgar was born on 23 September 1892 and baptised in Thornhill Church on 29 October 1892.

By 1911 Edgar and his father were boarders in the household of Frank and Charlotte Walker at Overton; both were working in the pit, John as a colliery lamp examiner and Edgar as a miner.

Edgar joined the colours with several other young men from Middlestown in November 1914: Willie P. Fox, Matthew Rhodes, William Parsons and George Jackson. (*Wakefield Express* 14 November 1914)

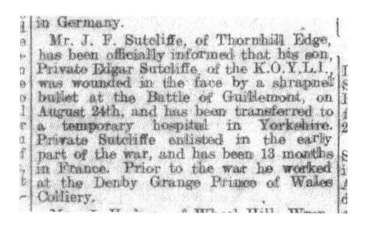

in Germany.

Mr. J. F. Sutcliffe, of Thornhill Edge, has been officially informed that his son, Private Edgar Sutcliffe, of the K.O.Y.L.I., was wounded in the face by a shrapnel bullet at the Battle of Guillemont, on August 24th, and has been transferred to a temporary hospital in Yorkshire. Private Sutcliffe enlisted in the early part of the war, and has been 13 months in France. Prior to the war he worked at the Denby Grange Prince of Wales Colliery.

Corporal Edgar Sutcliffe, son of Mrs. Mary Sutcliffe, of 3, Winn St., Barnsley, was aged 25 years old when he was killed on the 4 October 1917 in the Battle of Broodseinde.

10th (Service) Battalion, KOYLI was formed at Pontefract in September 1914 as part of K3 and came under command of 64th Brigade in 21st Division. The Battalion moved to Berkhamsted and then to Halton Park (Tring) in

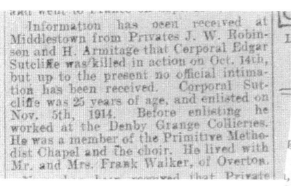

Information has been received at Middlestown from Privates J. W. Robinson and H. Armitage that Corporal Edgar Sutcliffe was killed in action on Oct. 14th, but up to the present no official intimation has been received. Corporal Sutcliffe was 25 years of age, and enlisted on Nov. 5th, 1914. Before enlisting he worked at the Denby Grange Collieries. He was a member of the Primitive Methodist Chapel and the choir. He lived with Mr. and Mrs. Frank Walker, of Overton.

Wakefield Express 20 October 1917

A MIDDLESTOWN SOLDIER'S DEATH.

ALWAYS THE FIRST TO VOLUNTEER FOR ANY DANGEROUS WORK.

Second-Lieutenant A. Walters, writing to Mrs. Sutcliffe, of Barnsley, in respect to the death of her son, Corporal Edgar Sutcliffe, formerly of Middlestown, says "He was killed in action on October 4, in the midst of severe fighting. It was a glorious indeed to see our noble lads inflict defeat upon the enemy, but we all paid the price of victory, and your most fearless boy, I was very sorry to hear had been killed, for we were going forward, and the fight was at its height when he was killed. He was my best N.C.O. and loved by me, and he was a great favourite with all the men of the company. He was always the first to volunteer for any dangerous work, and he gloried in doing his utmost to put the fighting spirit into the men. I had only known him a short time, but he filled me with admiration by the way he used to perform his duties."

Gunner Hubert Inman, youngest son of Mr. and Mrs. Alfred Inman, of Overton, is in the Second Australian Hospital, France, suffering from a wound in the ankle.

Private T. Broderick, West Yorkshire

October 1914, going on to billets in Maidenhead in November. They returned to Halton Park in April 1915 and went on to Witley in August. In September 1915, they landed in France on the 13 February 1918 the battalion was disbanded in France, with at least some of the men going to 20th Entrenching Battalion.

The Battle of Broodseinde was fought on 4 October 1917 near Ypres in Flanders, at the east end of the Gheluvelt plateau, by the British Second and Fifth armies and the German 4th Army. The

Wakefield Express 3 November 1917

battle was the most successful Allied attack of the Battle of Passchendaele. Using "bite-and-hold" tactics, with objectives limited to what could be held against German counter-attacks, the British devastated the German defence, which prompted a crisis among the German commanders and caused a severe loss of morale in the German 4th Army. Preparations were made by the Germans for local withdrawals and planning began for a greater withdrawal, which would entail the loss for the Germans of the Belgian coast, one of the strategic aims of the British offensive.

On 4 October 1917, 10th Battalion, KOYLI, during the Battle of Broodseinde, was involved in an attack to seize a portion of road just west of Reutel with the second objective (not reached) being the village of Reutel itself within the Ypres Salient.

The 21st Division had 2,616 casualties, the highest loss of a Second Army division, including Corporal Edgar Sutcliffe who was killed in action. He has no known grave but is remembered at Tyne Cot and on the war memorial in St Luke's Church, Overton.

Private Rowland Kaye
2nd Battn
KOYLI
30941

The son of coal miner Seth Kaye and his wife Martha Ann (nee Sykes), Rowland was born in Flockton, the younger brother of Mary Ann.

On 3 October 1905, in the Ebenezer Chapel, Turnpike Road, Horbury, Rowland married Edna Walker, the daughter of William Walker, a coal miner and his wife Clara. At the time of the wedding, Rowland, then aged 25, was a master grocer, living at 48, Derbyshire Street, Hunslet, Leeds and Edna, aged 22, was a rag sorter, living in Walkers' Buildings, Middlestown.

By 1911, Rowland and Edna, together with their one year old daughter Phillis, were living in Middlestown and Rowland was employed as a coal miner.

June, 1910, to August, 1917."
A MEMORIAL SERVICE in memory of Pte. Rowland Kaye (who was killed in France early in December last) took place at the Primitive Methodist Chapel on Sunday evening. The Rev. F. M. Ridge conducted the service, and preached a very impressive sermon. He referred to the good and faithful services the deceased had rendered to the chapel, he having been a member for nineteen years. He also held the position of organist for a long period, besides holding other offices both at the chapel and the Sunday School. Favourite hymns of the deceased were sung by request. Miss Linda Ward also sang a solo. There was a large congregation. Mr. Rufus Hutchinson, the organist, tastefully played "O Rest in the Lord" and the "Dead March" (Saul).

Wakefield Express 22 December 1917

Tyne Cot

The family grew and by the time of his enlistment in Ossett, Rowland was a father of four, working for Prudential Assurance Limited. He was the organist at Middlestown Primitive Methodist Chapel and a Sunday School teacher.

Rowland died on the 2 December 1917 during night action in the Battle of Passchendaele; he was 37 years old. He is buried at grave reference 111 H 11 at the Tyne Cot Cemetery. A memorial service was held in Middlestown Methodist Chapel, which Rowland had attended for nineteen years and at which he was the organist.

Lance Corporal George Kitchen
King's Own Yorkshire Light Infantry
2nd & 6th Battalion
Regimental Number 235140

When George Kitchen was born on 10 March 1889 in Netherton, Yorkshire, his father, Richard, was 31 and his mother, Charlotte, was 29. He was their fourth child and would eventually have seven brothers and two sisters. At about six weeks old, George was baptised at the Wesleyan Methodist Chapel in Netherton on the 28 May 1889.

The family was living in Cluntergate, Horbury in 1891, but by 1901 had moved to Bulling Balk Lane, Horbury Junction and in 1911 their address was Spring End, Horbury and George was working as a miner at Hartley Bank Colliery.

On 20 May 1911 George married Hannah Elizabeth Newton at St Michael and All Angels Church in Thornhill; George was twenty-two years old and Hannah just eighteen. Hannah came from Middlestown and the couple went to live at New Scarborough, Netherton. There do not appear to be any children born to Hannah and George.

George was in the Territorials and was called up at the start of the war. This is his account of an incident in the trenches in August 1915:

Within a month George was back in the firing line:

Wakefield Express 11 September 1915

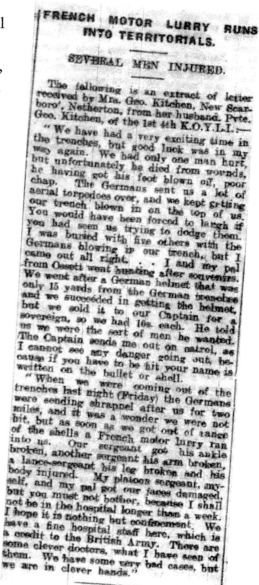

FRENCH MOTOR LURRY RUNS INTO TERRITORIALS.

SEVERAL MEN INJURED.

The following is an extract of letter received by Mrs. Geo. Kitchen, New Scarboro', Netherton, from her husband, Pvte. Geo. Kitchen, of the 1st 4th K.O.Y.L.I.:—

"We have had a very exciting time in the trenches, but good luck was in my way again. We had only one man hurt, but unfortunately he died from wounds, poor chap. The Germans sent us a lot of aerial torpedoes over, and we kept getting our trench blown in on the top of us. You would have been forced to laugh if you had seen us trying to dodge them. I was buried with five others with the Germans blowing up our trench, but I came out all right. . . I and my pal from Ossett went hunting after souvenirs. We went after a German helmet that was only 15 yards from the German trenches and we succeeded in getting the helmet, but we sold it to our Captain for a sovereign, so we had 10s. each. He told us we were the sort of men he wanted. The Captain sends me out on patrol, as I cannot see any danger going out, because if you have to be hit your name is written on the bullet or shell.

"When we were coming out of the trenches last night (Friday) the Germans were sending shrapnel after us for two miles, and it was a wonder we were not hit, but as soon as we got out of range of the shells a French motor lurry ran into us. Our sergeant got his ankle broken, another sergeant his arm broken, a lance-sergeant his leg broken and his body injured. My platoon sergeant, myself, and my pal got our faces damaged, but you must not bother, because I shall not be in the hospital longer than a week. I hope it is nothing but confinement. We have a fine hospital staff here, which is a credit to the British Army. There are some clever doctors, what I have seen of them. We have some very bad cases, but we are in clever hands."

Wakefield Express 21 August 1915

Later that year he was one of several local men who were victims of a gas attack in December 1915.

He was out of action for many months before returning to the front line in January 1917.

On 9 September 1917 George was admitted to the No 2 Canadian Casualty Clearing Station with pyrexia of unknown origin and trench fever. From early on in World War I, men started falling ill to a mysterious debilitating illness. Up to a third of British troops seen by doctors during the war were thought to have been suffering with the disease. The initial symptoms of the illness were generally short-lived, but recovery was often slow taking several months. Complications included relapses of the illness (as much

Wakefield Express 1 January 1916

as 10 years after the initial bout), heart problems, fatigue, anxiety, and depression. The name given to the condition was trench fever, but despite naming it, the doctors had no definite idea of what caused it. Only after the war was the cause discovered: bacteria carried by body lice.

George was transferred to Number 6 Convalescent Depot on 23 September 1917. He again returned to the front line, but was killed on 16 December 1917. He was with six other soldiers in a shelter when the shelling started. The first shells passed overhead, but eventually one struck the shelter, burying the men and killing four of them, including twenty-eight year old Lance-Corporal George Kitchen. He is remembered on the war memorial in St Andrew's Church, Netherton and on the memorial at Tyne Cot.

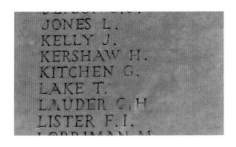

Like many young war widows, Hannah Elizabeth went on to marry again. On 10 January 1920 she married George Edward Ridsdale at St Luke's Church in Middlestown. George was a labourer and witnesses at the wedding were Hannah's brother and Ada Wiper.

KOYLI Memorial, Tyne Cot

Wakefield Express 19 January 1918

George's brother Tom also died in the Great War. He served in the 7th Battalion of the Lincolnshire Regiment (Reg. no 10455) and died from penetrating wounds gained during the Battle of the Somme on 16 July 1916.

1918

Private Brooke Bottomley
12 Battalion KOYLI
12/1980

Brooke Bottomley was born in Dewsbury Moor, *c* 1881, the son of Fenton and Emma Bottomley. A coal miner, Brooke married Agnes Dyson, aged 23, the daughter of Harry Dyson, a labourer, on 27 June 1903 in Mirfield Parish Church. The family lived in three rooms in Quarry Buildings, Wellhouse Lane, Mirfield and there raised three children, Nora (born 1906), Mary (born 1909) and Arthur (born 1911), all of whom were baptised in St Mary's Church, Mirfield.

It is thought that Private Brooke Bottomley was wounded and then subsequently died in May during the defence of the Nieppe Forest on the 13 April 1918. The KOYLI 12th Battalion was attached to 31 Division as their Pioneer Corps, i.e. tasked with work such as digging trenches. In their kit, they carried a pick for this work and fewer rounds of ammunition than normal infantry soldiers.

At least four German Divisions of the 6th Army attacked the Nieppe Forest towards Hazebrouck on the 13 April, but made little progress until late afternoon. This is the tactical incident referred to in the official history as "The Defence of the Nieppe Forest" and is the first of the two major German attacks of the day. This sector directly covered Hazebrouck; an area lying approximately between Merville and Merris, centred on Vieux Berquin. This was held by the left wing of 95 Brigade (50th Division), 4 Guards Brigade (31st Division), remnants of 86th and 87th Brigade (29th Division), holding less than 1,000 yards, and also 92nd Brigade (31st Division) with remnants of 92nd and 93rd Brigades attached as composite battalions. The 4th Guards Brigade with 12/KOYLI (attached pioneers of the 31st Division) took the worst of this prolonged German assault. At the height of the fighting the greater part of three German Divisions attacked the 4,000 yard front held by 4th Guards and adjacent units.

Brooke was 37 when he was killed on 12 May 1918; he is buried in the Anzac Cemetery, Sailly-Sur-La-Lys and commemorated on the war memorial in St Luke's Church, Overton.

Brooke left a widow and three young children, by then living at 6 Church Terrace, Middlestown. Agnes

Bottomley inherited Brooke's effects and received war grants of £19-10s-8d and £15-10s.

In due course Agnes married again; her bridegroom in St Luke's Church on 20 August 1921 was James Beaumont of Highfield Terrace, Middlestown.

Gunner Ernest Froggatt
RFA L/1201

Ernest Froggatt was born in Thornhill, the (Grand)son of George and Charlotte Froggatt, Overton

In 1911 the family was living at Caphouse, Overton and in April 1917, by then employed at Denby Grange Colliery, following recruiting meetings in the parish, Ernest along with Hubert Inman and Herbert Armitage, joined the Wakefield Artillery Battery of the 161st Battery.

Gunner Ernest Froggett died on the 25 April 1918 during the 2nd Battle of Kemmel Ridge.

50th Brigade RFA was originally comprised of numbers 160, 161 and 162 Batteries RFA and the Brigade Ammunition Column. It was placed under command of the 9th (Scottish) Division and went to France with it in May 1915.

In February 1915 the three six-gun batteries were reorganised to become four four-gun batteries and were titled as A, B, C and D.

On 21 February 1916 D Battery left to join 53 Brigade of the same Division, being replaced by the former B (Howitzer) Battery of that brigade which now became D/50.

On 8 September 1916, A and B were increased to six guns

RECRUITING MEETINGS.

Recruiting campaigns took place on Monday evening at the Town End, Middlestown; near the Church, Flockton; The Cross, Emley; near the Black Bull Inn, Midgley; Town End, Netherton; and at Horbury Bridge, when speeches and appeals for recruits were made by Mr. A. H. Marshall, M.P., Mr. Cecil L. Kaye, D.L., Mr. J. T. Mills (Wakefield), Mr. Garrett, Mr. C. J. Haworth, and other gentlemen.

It was explained that a new battery to be known as the 164th battery or the Wakefield Battery was to be formed. In respect to the latter all would be aware that Wakefield had been made into a County Borough, and an appeal had been made to the Mayor by Lord Kitchener to try and form a battery which would be known both now and in future as the Wakefield Battery.

A company of Boy Scouts, with bugles and drums, paraded the villages, and at each meeting there were a large number of people present, and the speeches by each of the above-named gentlemen were very much appreciated.

Wakefield Express 17 April 1915 p11

of wounds on April 19th.
GUNNER ERNEST FROGGATT, of Overton, has died in hospital after having been severely wounded. The official news was received by his grandmother, Mrs. Froggatt, Caphouse, Overton. Froggatt, who was only twenty years of age, was attached to the Royal Field Artillery, and had been several times commended for ... excellent ... He enlisted just over three years ago, and had been in France about 2½ years, during which time he was twice gassed. Before enlisting he worked at Denby Grange Collieries.

DRIVER W. ILLINGWORTH, Royal

Wakefield Express 1 June 1918 p6

when joined by sections from B Battery of 53 Brigade, and the same happened to C Battery which was joined by a section from C/53.

Two howitzers made D Battery up to six when a section joined from D/52 on 9 January 1917.

In 1918 they fought on the Somme, in the Battles of the Lys and The Advance in Flanders, capturing the Outtersteene Ridge and seeing action in the Battle of Courtrai and the action of Ooteghem. They were resting in billets at the Armistice.

On April 25 and 26 1918, the 21st Division was involved in a ferocious battle, the 2nd Battle of Kemmel (or the Kemmelberg), part of the Battle of the Lys, in order to prevent a German attack getting round behind Ypres from the South. A joint French and British action was organised for the 25 April with the objective of taking the Vierstraat Line.

At the start of the battle, at 02:30 hours, on 25 April 1918, over 250 batteries of German guns opened up on Allied artillery positions with a mixture of gas and high explosive. For the next two hours they concentrated solely on destroying gun emplacements. It was during this bombardment that Gunner Ernest Froggett lost his life.

Gunner Froggett is remembered on the war memorial in St Luke's Church, Overton and on the memorial to the missing at Tyne Cot, Belgium. His sole legatee was his mother, Charlotte Froggett.

Lance Corporal Wilfred Bowers (1899 - 1918)
Prince of Wales Own (West Yorkshire)
15th Regiment
Regimental Number 43355

When Wilfred Bowers and his twin brother William were born on 29 March 1899 in Netherton, their father, Walter, was 39 and their mother, Frances, was 35. Wilfred already had eight brothers and three sisters. The Bowers family was a well-known local family, all of whom were born in Netherton. Wilfred and William were baptised on 4 March 1899 at Trinity Methodist Chapel, Netherton.

Wilfred and William were enrolled at St Andrew's School, near St Andrew's Church, Netherton on 2 April 1906.

By 1911 census, eleven members of the family were living in a house on Stockstone Terrace, Netherton and the boys were working in the pit.

By the time of his enlistment in the 'Leeds Pals' in Pontefract on 27 April 1917, 18 year old Wilfred was employed as a clothdresser.

Netherton School is shown to the left of the church

Stockstone Terrace,
Netherton

The "Leeds Pals" 15th (Service) Battalion (1st Leeds) was formed in Leeds in September 1914 by the Lord Mayor and City. In June 1915 the formation came under orders of 93rd Brigade, 31st Division and in December 1915 they moved to Egypt. The battalion went on to France in March 1916. On the 7 December 1917 they amalgamated with 17th Battalion to form the 15th/17th Battalion.

In 1918, the battalion fought at the Battle of St Quentin, The Battle of Bapaume, The First Battle of Arras, The Battle of Estaires, The Battle of Hazebrouck, The Defence of Nieppe Forest, The attack at La Becque, The capture of Vieux Berquin, The Battle of Ypres, the action of Tieghem and ended the war at Renaix, Belgium. Lance Corporal Bowers was most probably wounded (possibly by friendly fire) during the Action at Le Becque on the 28 June 1918.

After the bitter fighting of the Battle of the Lys had ended with the failure of the German Army to break through to Hazebrouck, the front lines in the Vieux Berquin sector were re-established in front of Aval Wood, on the eastern fringe of the Nieppe Forest.

On 28 June 1918, 5th and 31st Divisions received orders to attack on a 6,000-yard (5.5km) front east of the Nieppe Forest. The operation was designed both to disrupt any plans the enemy might have for a renewed offensive, and to push the British lines away from the edge of the wood where they had made an easy target for hostile artillery.

In a night time operation aimed at securing a position from which enfilade fire could be used to support the main attack, two companies of the 13th York & Lancasters supported by part of two companies of the 18th Durham Light Infantry captured Ankle Farm in the early morning of 27 June. Later that day the main attack was practiced by 92nd Brigade (31st Division) in the area of la Papote, some 3½ miles (5-6km) behind the front line.

In one of many contrasts to the opening day of the Battle of the Somme two years previously, the enemy were not to be forewarned of the attack by a preliminary artillery bombardment. The attacking troops reached their assembly trenches in the quiet early hours of the 28th, unnoticed by the enemy.

At the far left of the 31st Division front, the 15th/17th West Yorkshires (Leeds Pals & Bantams) of 93rd Brigade were to capture and consolidate la Becque Farm (from which the action takes its name) before pushing on to Plate Becque stream.

On the left of the attack, the 15th/17th West Yorkshires encountered only isolated pockets of resistance in driving through to their objectives under the protection of the creeping barrage. In circumstances that were repeated along the length of the front, attacking troops pressing too closely to the barrage were inevitably hit by their own shrapnel, accounting for many of the battalion's 170 casualties.

Wilfred died from his wounds aged 19 years old on Thursday 11 July 1918. He is mentioned on three local memorial plaques – one in St Andrew's Church in Netherton, one in Trinity Methodist Church, Netherton (which describes him as a Private and the other in Netherton School.

From the plaque in the school, it appears that Wilfred's twin William survived. A detailed description of the school's war memorial unveiling, which was attended by Wilfred's parents, appears on pages 68–71.

Wilfred is buried in the Longuenesse Souvenir Cemetery in Pas de Calais, France (Plot V C 64 Memorial ID 56600906)

Wilfred was also remembered as part of the installation at the Tower of London when his great niece, Audrey Parker successfully submitted Wilfred's name to be included in the Roll of Honour ceremonies and also purchased one of the Tower of London poppies in his memory.

Private Harry Lee (1892 - 1918)
Kings Own Yorkshire Light Infantry
1st / 4th Battalion
Regimental Number 201037

Harry, the son of Lister, a miner, and his wife Sarah Jane Lee was baptised at St Luke's Church, Middlestown on 4 February 1892.

By 1911, the family were living at the Old Oil Mill in Horbury Bridge

Reid's Oil Mill & Chimney can be seen to the right of this photograph and this is the area where the Lee family would have lived.

Robert Reid was a successful business man – making his fortune through the family business of J Reid & Sons, Oil & Grease Distillers. Robert was referred to locally as Millionaire Reid. Raw wool used in the woollen manufacturing industry

Reid's Mill

Drill Hall, Ossett

had to be scoured to remove the grease before it could be used in the spinning of yarn. Reids used the by-products of this process, the oil, to manufacture lubrication grease for making polishes used in the leather industry.

Along with many other local lads Harry enlisted here in Ossett. We believe that the majority of these men served in the 1/4 Battalion of the King's Own Yorkshire Light Infantry, and specifically 'D' Company, which was largely made up of men from Ossett and Horbury.

In effect, a group of *"Ossett Pals"* who trained, fought and died together. Many of these men were gassed in their trenches in late December 1915 and many more died on the beaches at Nieuport on the Belgian coast, near Ostend in July 1917. All these men were 'Saturday Soldiers' or Territorials.

Those men from the Territorial force who had not signed up for overseas service became part of the 2nd/4th Battalion, King's Own Yorkshire Light Infantry, and were designated for home service, but they too were soon to find that they were needed on the Western Front and were eventually sent to fight in France.

Life in the trenches was summed up by the phrase which later became well-known: "Months of boredom punctuated by moments of extreme terror."

From the 1/4 Battalion War Diary, there were no battles during September 1918 involving the battalion. They had been holding the Front Line near Ypres and on the 1 September, they moved by bus from Framecourt to the Chateau de la Haie area and St. Lawrence Camp.

On the 2 September, they moved by route march to Blagny for training and then marched back to St. Lawrence Camp for more training. On the 13 September, the battalion moved back to the Front Line near Ypres. Whilst holding the line, there were two casualties from wounding on the 14 September and one more on the 15 September.

Harry Lee is buried in the Aubugny Communal Cemetery Extension, IV.B.31

Wakefield Express 28 September 1918

Corporal Freddie Morley
York and Lancaster Regiment
204535

Freddie was the second Son of Albert and Elizabeth Morley, nee Littlewood. At the time of their marriage at St Luke's Church, Middlestown on 12 October 1889, Albert was a miner.

Freddie was brought up on Overton Farm and joined up in March 1916.

Corporal Freddie Morley, aged 21 years, of Manor Farm, Flockton, Wakefield, died on the 13 October 1918 in the action known as the "Pursuit to the Selle."

Wakefield Express

The 1/5 Battalion was formed in Rotherham in August 1914 and was part of 3rd West Riding Brigade, West Riding Division. The formation moved on mobilisation to Doncaster, and again in November 1914 to Gainsborough, going on in February 1915 to York. On the 14 April 1915 they landed at Boulogne. On the 15 May 1915 the formation became 148th Brigade in 49th (West Riding) Division.

The Pursuit to the Selle was an official title given to the actions of the 1st, 3rd and 4th armies in driving the Germans back to the River Selle when the 49th Division was heavily involved in this action.

The 49th Division were on the right flank of First Army's drive on the 11 October. They had been deployed to XXII Corps from GHQ Reserve (VIII Corps) on the 10th October, replacing the right side of the 2nd Canadian Division in the line on the night of 10/11 October. On the 11 October both divisions attacked as part of the Canadian Corps' critical role of protecting the left flank of Third Army. Their objective was the line (Right to Left/South to North) Saulzoir (49th Division)--Avesnes le Sec-Lieu St. Amand. On the 11 October they encountered severe resistance after a quiet start, surprising the Germans with a late jump-off (09.00), and were forced to retire over open ground in face of infantry, artillery and tank attacks. Casualties were very high. It was here that Corporal Freddie Morley lost his life.

Freddie is buried in the York Cemetery, Haspres and is remembered on the war memorial in St Luke's Church, Overton.

**Private Ray Alfred Blythe
Kings Own Yorkshire Light Infantry
1/5, 10th and 1st / 4th Battalions
Regimental Number 205564**

Ray Blythe was born in 1888 in North Newbald, East Yorkshire, when his father, George, would have been twenty-four years old and his mother, Mary, 26. He was the third of four siblings and had two brothers and one sister.

Ray was baptised on the 25 November 1888 at St Nicholas' Church in North Newbald

By the 1911 Census, Ray was living away from his home village and boarding with the Ashton family in 2 King's Yard, King Street, Horbury Bridge. He was now aged 22 and working as a carter - a general carrier. The Ashton family comprised of husband, wife, two sons and a daughter. It would have been rather a squash with six people living in just three rooms.

Hartley Bank Colliery

King Street is on the left hand side of Storrs Hill Road and today mainly comprises a row of terraced houses.

We know from the *Wakefield Express* that Ray worked as a farm labourer for Farmer F. Mosley in Middlestown and then worked at Hartley Bank Colliery. He possibly moved to New Scarborough in Netherton where many of the mine workers lived, so that he would be nearer the mine.

In August 1914, at the start of the war, whilst working at Hartley Bank Colliery, Ray enlisted at Wakefield into the Kings Own Yorkshire Infantry (KOYLI).

In April of 1918, the *Wakefield Express* reported that he was wounded. On November 2 1918, he was killed in action. Aged just 30 years and only nine days before peace was declared.

Private Ray Blythe is commemorated on the Vis-en-Artois Memorial, in his home town of North Newbald, with his name listed on both the Church and Cemetery War Memorials as well as on the war memorial in St Andrew's Church, Netherton.

WOUNDED SOLDIERS.—The following are among the soldiers who have been wounded in the recent fighting:— Pte. Wray Blythe, New Scarboro', Netherton; Pte. Frank Earnshaw, son of Cr. and Mrs. Reuben Earnshaw (Midgley), who is in a Brighton hospital suffering from shrapnel wounds in the knee and calf of the leg; Pte. W. Frost, Sandy-lane, Middlestown, severely wounded in the shoulder; Pte. Cecil Marsden, Middlestown, reported wounded in last week's "Express," is suffering from a shrapnel wound in the head.

The Vis-en-Artois Memorial commemorates 9,847 Allied officers and men who were killed in the period from 8 August 1918 to 11 November 1918. The battle period is known by the Allies as the "Advance to Victory". This was a series of battles fought in Picardy and Artois during the last months of the war, when the Allied Forces successfully pushed the German Army eastwards as far as Mons over the Belgian border. The men commemorated on this memorial have no known grave. They are from the Armies of Great Britain, Ireland and South Africa.

The memorial is located at the northern end of the Vis-en-Artois British Cemetery. It comprises two 70 foot high pylons with the Stone of Remembrance in the centre section between them, and a wing on either side of the centre section containing the names of the fallen.

Wakefield Express
14 December 1918 p1

A sculpted relief of St. George and the Dragon is located on the wall behind the Stone of Remembrance.

in France two years and six months. PVTE WRAY BLYTHE, K.O.Y.L.I., of Netherton, was killed in France on the 7th inst. At the time of enlisting he was working at the Hartley Bank Colliery, and previously he was in the employ of Mr. F Mosley, farmer, Middlestown. SECOND-LIEUT FRANK R OXLEY.

Private Blythe was the last man from the parish to die before the Armistice, which was agreed nine days after his death.

The Vis-en-Artois Memorial commemorates 9,847 Allied officers and men who were killed in the period from 8 August 1918 to 11 November 1918. The battle period is known by the Allies as the "Advance to Victory". This was a series of battles fought in Picardy and Artois during the last months of the war, when the Allied Forces successfully pushed the German

Army eastwards as far as Mons over the Belgian border. The men commemorated on this memorial have no known grave. They are from the Armies of Great Britain, Ireland and South Africa. The memorial is located at

Vis-en-Artois, British Cemetery

the northern end of the Vis-en-Artois British Cemetery. It comprises two 70 foot high pylons with the Stone of Remembrance in the centre section between them, and a wing on either side of the centre section containing the names of the fallen.

Private Percy Rooke Littlewood
Leicestershire Regiment
37840

Percy Rooke was the son of George and Emma Littlewood, nee Rooke. His mother Emma's family came from Bole in Nottinghamshire.

George Littlewood, a house painter, was from Middlestown and after his marriage to Emma he continued to live in the village. Percy Rooke was baptised in St Luke's Church on 2 March 1885.

In 1901 the family was living at New Road Side, Middlestown and Percy Rooke Littlewood was an apprentice mason.

By 1911 the family was living at Wickentree Hall, Sandy Lane, Middlestown and Percy Rooke was employed as an Attendant at Prestwich Asylum in Manchester.

He married Alice M. Smith in Eccleshall, Sheffield in December 1916.

Enlisted in Manchester into the 1st battalion, the Leicestershire Regiment. His service number was 37840

MIDDLESTOWN SOLDIER DIES OF WOUNDS.

Private Percy Rooke Littlewood, Royal Engineers, of Middlestown, died yesterday morning week at the British Red Cross Hospital, Bellahouston, near Glasgow, from wounds received in action in France on September 30th, when he had his knee shattered by an explosive bullet. He was on the battlefield for fully twelve hours before first-aid could be rendered. After being in a French hospital for a fortnight, he was removed to the hospital at Glasgow, where he underwent four operations, death taking place as above stated.

Deceased, who was 33 years of age, and who in civil life was a builder, enlisted about three years ago, and he had been in France about two years. He leaves a widow. The news of his death came as a great shock to many people in the village, as he was a man who was very highly respected.

The body was conveyed to Middlestown on Saturday night, and the funeral took place at Thornhill Church on Monday, when eight soldiers, who were home on furlough, officiated as bearers, whilst a number of discharged sailors and soldiers joined in the solemn procession to the church. The soldiers were in charge of Sergt. Harold Wardle, a Middlestown young man, and they marched from the Moulder's Arms, the headquarters of the Discharged Sailors and Soldiers' Association. The Rev. A. E. Hey officiated at the funeral.

Wakefield Express
21 December 1918

Percy Rooke's death was caused by wounds received in action on 30 September 1918. After twelve hours on the battlefield waiting to be rescued, Percy Rooke was taken to a French hospital. After two weeks he was evacuated to the United Kingdom and died at Bellahouston Red Cross Hospital, Glasgow, on 13 December 1918; he was aged 33 and left behind his wife Alice.

His body was brought back to Middlestown and a military funeral arranged, with the burial in Thornhill churchyard. (Thornhill was the mother church of the ancient parish and the Cemetery at Middlestown was not created until 1930).

DEDICATION OF THE ST LUKE'S WAR MEMORIAL IN 1920

Hilary Haigh

ST. LUKE'S CHURCH

A SHORT TIME ago a committee representing practically all denominations in the village met and discussed the idea of erecting a memorial in memory of the men of Middlestown and Overton who fell in the Great European War. To the regret of many, nothing was decided upon. After the many suggestions made, however, the members of the above church were anxious to honour the lads who had fallen, a subscription list was opened and soon the necessary money was forthcoming. It was decided that the most suitable memorial would be a stained glass window, and this has been put in on the south side of the church and inscribed 'To the glory of God and in grateful remembrance of the noble sacrifice of the following men who gave their lives for King and country in the Great War, 1914-19, this tablet and adjacent window are erected by members of this church',

The handsome brass tablet erected close to the window bears the following names of the fallen heroes from the village:-

C C. Bedford, W.H.Bedford, B.Bottomley, H. Davies, J.Dunn, E. Froggatt, W.Gill, W. Hooper, B. Howden, H. Howden, R. Kaye, W. Kaye, P. R. Littlewood, F. Morley, T. Sanders, R. J. Schooling, L. Shires, R.E. Stubbs, E. Sutcliffe and W. Taylor.

The dedication took place on Saturday afternoon, of this and another window erected in memory of Signaller Wilfred Kaye, who fell in action on Passchendaele Ridge October 9th 1917, aged 28 years. 'This window is dedicated by his mother and sisters'.

The windows and tablet were unveiled by the Rev. L.N. Hodges, Vicar of Holmfirth and formerly Vicar of Middlestown, who was during the war a chaplain to H. M. Forces. The dedication was performed by the Archdeacon of Huddersfield (Ven. R. C. M. Harvey). It was a very impressive service and during the time the dedication was being performed the choir, who stood at each side of the memorials, sang the hymn 'The Supreme Sacrifice', which is a special hymn for these occasions.

After the ceremony, the choir, headed by the Cross, marched back to their places, singing the hymn, 'Jesus lives, no longer now', and after special responses had been said, together with suitable collects, the Archdeacon preached a most impressive sermon from the words 'Consider the issue of their lives and imitate their faith'.

He said they had met together on a very solemn occasion and it would no doubt bring back to memory thoughts of the ones who had been lost. He spoke also of the true comradeship shown by the men during the War, and by men of practically all nations, when they were face to face with a common enemy.

This was one of the things struck us all lost forcibly together with the loyalty shown by all ranks to their leaders. True comradeship was an essential thing in getting peace in our industrial affairs, unrest being now very prevalent. If more of this spirit were shown, instead of the employers and employees holding daggers at each others' throats, peace would quickly reign. It appeared as though we had not yet learnt the lesson which the years of the late war should have taught us.

The windows are representations of St Aidan and St Wilfred respectively. The collection gathered £4-9s-6d, which will be applied towards filling the south side with another window on a future occasion, as there is now only one half of a window left that is not stained glass.

A number of beautiful floral tributes were sent, and after the service these were placed near the memorials.

Among the large congregation were members of the families of the fallen soldiers, as well as a number of ex-soldiers who served during the War, and for each of them seats were reserved.

Wakefield Express 2 October 1920

ST LUKE'S, OVERTON WAR MEMORIAL WINDOWS CONSERVATION

Adam Goodyear

IN THE EARLY 1970s, with the closure and subsequent demolition of St Luke's, Middlestown the stained glass windows were removed including the three WW1 memorial windows by the London studio founded by Charles Eamer Kempe.

By the time of their conservation the windows were approaching 100 years old. There is a very crude rule of thumb that a stained glass window will need re-leading every 100 – 150 years. This depends upon many things, the quality of the original build, whether the window is in an exposed or sheltered location and the number of saddle bars which support the window. The windows were generally in good condition they had been supplied with many saddle bars and so whatever the elements had thrown at them they were able to withstand. The one area where they had universally suffered was in the narrow tinted border known as a "fillet" which traditionally surrounds a stained glass window. It is included in a design to provide a sacrificial area which can be broken if a window has to be removed so avoiding damage to the important subject areas.

One would hope that any studio today would aim to remove a window without causing any damage, it preserves all the original glass intact, even the mundane and saves time selecting and cutting new glass. Whoever removed the Kempe windows, whether due to a lack of time or knowledge took the concept of a "sacrificial border" quite literally. Not one piece of the fillet in any of the three windows survived unbroken or even complete.

The first process of the conservation project was to photograph all the panels in their original state. Had the windows been in poorer condition and re-leading was required the next process would have been to lay a sheet of very thin paper over each panel and with a wax block make a rubbing of the leads akin to a brass rubbing. This records the positions of all the leads prior to dismantling the panels. As only the outer leads, the glass of the fillet and the lead which divided the fillet from the subject area were to be replaced there was no need for a rubbing, a series of measurements provided the details required to exactly rebuild these areas.

Having removed the two leads and the broken fillet, new glass which matched the tint and texture of the original was selected. All other glass in the windows is handmade, mouthblown "antique " glass however the fillet is what is known as "cathedral" glass, that is, a machine made textured glass. New leads were selected which accurately replicated the original in both size and profile.

The cleaning of stained glass is a very delicate operation and the approach depends upon how well the glass painting has been fired. During the painting process the glass is fired a number of times and at a temperature which allows the upper surface to become molten and so absorb the glass paint. Once cooled the paint will have thoroughly bonded with the glass and it will have a shiny surface. Nothing short of acid will now remove the paint. If however a sufficient temperature has not been reached the paint will lay on the surface like a crust, it will have a matt appearance and in time even condensation will remove the paint. Fortunately these windows, like most Kempe windows of this period, were well fired and the paint has a very glossy appearance. The panels were cleaned by first gently brushing away the loose dust with a soft paint brush. The inner painted surface was then cleaned with cotton wool swabs dampened with de-ionised water. The outer surface was cleaned with a fibreglass brush.

With the cleaning process complete the new fillets were leaded in place and the new leading soldered. The newly built areas were sealed with "leaded light cement" a putty based substance with the addition of red lead, linseed oil

Adam Goodyear

and "lamp black" to darken it. It is of a creamy consistency and can be brushed under the leads. Once hard it makes the panels rigid and weatherproofs them.

Considering the age of the windows there were very few cracks and most were minor and unobtrusive. If the panels were being re-leaded these would have been edge bonded however as the windows were to be mounted inside, water ingress was not a concern. The few cracks which were more obvious had fine face leads soldered over them. The one area of serious damage was to the dedication in the St Oswald window. There were a number of cracks and one piece was missing. By edge bonding the cracks and painting a new piece for the missing area the rest of the original dedication could be preserved.

The next process was to once again photograph the panels and produce a diagram of each panel indicating where new glass and lead had been used and where cracks had been edge bonded. Along with a conservation report this provides a record of all works undertaken. The only thing left to do was to fit the new light box and install the windows.

THE KEMPE WAR MEMORIAL WINDOWS FROM ST. LUKE'S, MIDDLESTOWN

Adrian Barlow

WHEN THE VICTORIAN church of St Luke, Middlestown, was declared unsafe and demolished in 1969-70, much of its stained glass was damaged. However, the surviving pieces were stored in a cupboard in the new St. Luke's church. Among these pieces were the remains of three windows which, together with a brass memorial plaque, had formed the original church's First World War memorial. The glass had come from the Studio of C.E. Kempe & Co, a firm established in 1907 after the death of the Studio's founder, Charles Eamer Kempe, the leading figure in late Victorian English church art and decoration. In 2016 the glass was fully restored and reassembled by stained glass conservator Adam Goodyear into a single three-light window now mounted in a light box and displayed on the wall of the new church. A study of this glass, and of its origins, sheds valuable light both on the work of the Kempe Studio and on attitudes to memorializing the Great War and its victims, both individually and collectively.

Although Charles Kempe (1837-1907) was a Sussex man whose Studio was located in London, he had been active in Yorkshire almost from the start of his career. One of his very first windows is the west window of the Holy Cross Chapel in Horbury's former House of Mercy (now Cliffe House School); between 1872-1875 he was commissioned to decorate the Chapel at Castle Howard, and during the same period be began the great scheme of windows in Wakefield Cathedral, which today has more windows by Kempe, created over a longer period, than any other Cathedral in Britain. A significant number of parish churches – large and small in and around Leeds, Bradford and Wakefield – can also boast 'stained glass by Kempe'.

It needs to be made clear, however, that Kempe glass is not the work of a single man. Kempe gathered around him artists and draughtsmen capable of designing windows, vestments and church furnishings such as reredoses in the style which he himself developed, based on late medieval examples of English, French and Flemish religious art. Expressive faces; elaborate vestments and garments richly decorated with pearls and jewels; sacred symbols and biblical texts – all these were the elements of what had come, by the end of the 19th century, to be instantly recognizable as hall marks of Kempe art. To achieve this, Kempe also brought together expert craftsmen who could realize the designs in stained glass, at every stage: cutting out the pieces of glass; painting and firing the pieces in the kiln; assembling them using lead 'cames' (strips of lead, H-shaped in cross-section) to create the complete window which then had to be assembled *in situ*, secure enough to withstand British weather for hundreds of years.

Demand for Kempe glass was so great that at its height the Studio was employing at least sixty men at its offices in Marylebone and its glassworks at Millbrook, in Camden Town. Yet all this work and every design was overseen by Kempe himself. Acknowledged within the Church of England as an expert on biblical and church history and as an authority on liturgy and ceremonial, as head of the Studio he resembled the conductor of a celebrated orchestra or the director of a theatre company with a distinctive style audiences had come to expect. Some of his windows are signed, occasionally with the Kempe shield (three wheatsheaves on a red background with a gold border) or, more commonly, with a single wheatsheaf, often found in the lower left-hand corner of a window. Wheatsheaves with a small black tower superimposed on them indicate that the window comes from C. E. Kempe & Co. The Tower indicates that the Chairman of the new company was Kempe's cousin and heir, Walter Ernest Tower. Production of windows at the Millbrook glassworks finally ceased in 1934.

There were four Kempe & Co. windows in the old St. Luke's Church, all of them in single lancets, so the shape and overall design is remarkably consistent. This gives an added unity to the three restored panels, now presented as one war memorial window; in their original settings the lancets would have been more

Joseph

widely spaced than they now appear. The earliest window (also restored and today displayed in the sanctuary of the new church) dates from 1909. It is important as a template for the later windows, but unusual and interesting in its own right. As with all the windows, it depicts a single figure, St. Joseph, though above and behind him two angels can be seen holding a 'Cloth of Honour'. This is bordered with pearls at the top and a fringe of tassels glimpsed at the bottom. 'Cloths of Honour', painted to resemble damask or rich brocade, are often found in Kempe windows, either seen behind the pale and dying body of Christ on the Cross in Crucifixion windows, or as a backdrop to scenes such as the Annunciation. Joseph himself is easily identified by the carpenter's set square he carries in his left hand; less obvious, however, is the significance of what he carries in his right. This looks, at first glance, like the conventional wooden staff an old man such as Joseph might carry but, surprisingly, from its head a spray of lilies is blooming.

What is going on? Kempe himself had delighted in such symbolism, and his Chief Draughtsman, John W. Lisle, had faithfully continued in this tradition after 1907. Nevertheless, Joseph's staff in this Middlestown window is unique: it refers to the biblical prophecy of Isaiah (*'And there shall come forth a rod out of the stem of Jesse, and a Branch shall grow out of his roots.'*) Joseph and Mary were both 'of the house and lineage of David', according to the gospel accounts of Matthew and Luke. So Joseph's staff represents the rod of Jesse, and the lilies are the symbol of purity always associated with Mary: a complex biblical allusion, therefore, expressed purely as a visual image.

The next window to be installed was dedicated in 1917, in memory of two brothers, Cecil and William Bedford, both killed on active service in 1916. Cecil died in Mesopotamia, and William was buried in a military cemetery in Rouen, having died of his wounds in hospital. One tends to think of war memorials as appearing only after the war was over; however, the decision of the British Government that all servicemen should be buried in the country where they died – no repatriation of the dead being permitted during either the First or the Second World War – meant that families who wished to commemorate their dead husbands / brothers / sons (and occasionally daughters, too) often turned to stained glass windows as a way of creating a memorial back in their home community. Such memorials, commemorating individual soldiers, or sailors lost at sea, began to appear as early as 1915.

Kempe himself had had no personal experience of war, but he admired the courage and dedication of soldiers. His brother had fought in the Crimea, surviving the Siege of Sebastopol (1854) and his brother-in-law had been killed during the Relief of Lucknow (1857); later in his life one of his closest friends had been Field Marshal Viscount Wolseley, Commander-in-Chief of British Forces. It was the South African War of 1899-1902 (the Boer War) that first created a demand for war memorial windows. Kempe preferred to treat such windows as a fit context for religious allegory rather than for literal depiction of war. Only one literal depiction survives (in a window in Shrewsbury School Chapel), but several windows from 1904 onwards personify the Virtues of Fortitude, Patience and Faithfulness – and Kempe's Virtues are always represented as women. By implication his windows conflate the idea of Soldiers of the Crown and Soldiers of Christ: one in Winchester Cathedral depicts Fortitude, seated on a throne, with Windsor Castle in the background, handing a Lee Enfield rifle to a kneeling soldier who wears British Army uniform of the period.

St. Oswald

Kempe himself may have come to feel uncomfortable about such heavy-handed symbolism. Later windows of his looked back to historical figures from much earlier British history who exemplified the combination of military and Christian heroism, and chief among these were two kings, St Edmund of East Anglia and St Oswald of Northumbria. In a window in Lichfield Cathedral, dedicated to the men of the South Staffordshire Regiment killed in South Africa, both these kings are shown alongside other royal saints and martyrs stretching back to St. George and St. Alban, the first English martyr, all of whom are gathered around an image of the Crucifixion.

In this window it is St Oswald who is at the foot of the Cross, and prominent among several texts inscribed in the window is the text 'Wilt thou lay down thy life for my sake?', Christ's challenge to Peter. In subsequent windows produced by the Kempe Studio and C.E. Kempe & Co. for churches and cathedrals throughout Britain and abroad, St Oswald becomes the embodiment of Christian kingly and Christian faithfulness combined. In the east window of Wakefield Cathedral, for instance, he is shown crowned and in armour, kneeling before the throne of Christ in Majesty. In one hand he holds the royal sceptre and in the other a tall, rugged cross.

This rugged cross, made from the trunk of a tree hastily cut down and shaped into a Cross on the eve of battle, to encourage his soldiers, is the emblem with

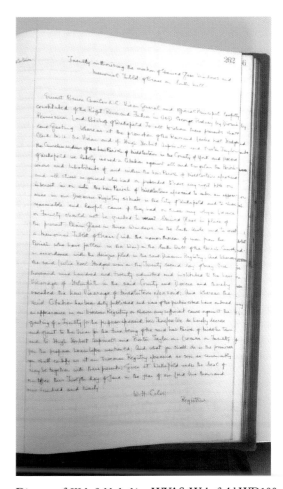

Diocese of *Wakefield Archive*, WYAS, Wakefield WD100

which St. Oswald is always depicted – as he is in the 1917 Middlestown window, designed by John Lisle. The battle in which Oswald was killed and his body dismembered was fought at Maserfield, traditionally identified as Oswestry (etymologically 'Oswald's Tree'). Oswald is celebrated not only as a Christian warrior but as the king who brought St. Aidan to become Bishop of Lindisfarne. Together with Aidan and Cuthbert, therefore, he is a central figure in the story of Christianity in the North of England. Thus, when the congregation of St. Luke's approached Kempe & Co. in 1920 for a war memorial window to commemorate all the dead of the parish, the proposal Lisle sketched for them showed three northern saints: Wilfrid, Aidan and Cuthbert. Lisle's sketch was duly forwarded to the Wakefield Diocesan Registrar, and the Faculty for the erection of the window and the accompanying brass Roll of Honour was granted in May. The Dedication of the window and the memorial plaque at a service on 25th September was reported in the *Wakefield Express* a week later, on 2nd October 1920.

What had been planned as a three-light window commemorating all the fallen of Middlestown was unveiled, however, only as two separate lancets. Behind this change of plan lay a story that was surprisingly common in post-First World War Britain: the impetus to create a war memorial was greater than the willingness of the community to pay for it. One of the two lights was paid

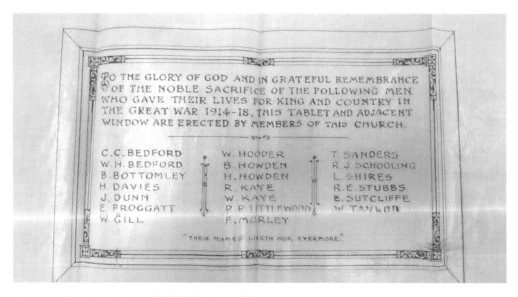

Diocese of *Wakefield Archive*, WYAS, Wakefield WD100

for by a single family, becoming a second private memorial alongside the Bedford family memorial; this one was given in memory of Private Wilfred Kaye, who had been killed at Passchendaele in 1917. Only the other light (St. Aidan) was, strictly speaking, the memorial to the men of Middlestown, and it was this one to which the inscription on the brass plaque referred: *'To the glory of God and in grateful remembrance of the noble sacrifice of the following men who gave their lives for King and country in the Great War, 1914-19, this tablet and adjacent window are erected by members of this church.'*

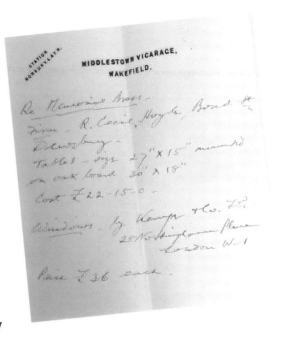

Diocese of *Wakefield Archive*, WYAS, Wakefield WD100

According to a note attached to the Faculty application, and written (presumably by the then Vicar of St. Luke's, the Rev. L.N. Hodges) on Middlestown Vicarage headed paper, Kempe & Co. had set the cost of each light at £36. A collection at the end of the Dedication service, on 25th September raised £4.9s.6d, which, the *Wakefield Express* announced, 'will be applied towards filling the south side with another window on a future occasion, as there is now only one half of a window left that is not stained glass.' This was therefore the intention: to raise a further £32 to fill the remaining light with the planned figure of St. Cuthbert. Evidently, however, with the service of Dedication over, and the list of names now permanently displayed on the brass plaque, the momentum had been lost and the money was simply not forthcoming.

Fifty years on, when the old St. Luke's was demolished, the War Memorial plaque was preserved but the glass – such of it as was not entirely broken – was roughly stored and forgotten in a cupboard. This is perhaps understandable: stained glass had long gone out of fashion. after a brief post-war revival, firms such as Kempe & Co. had closed back in the 1930s when demand for stained glass

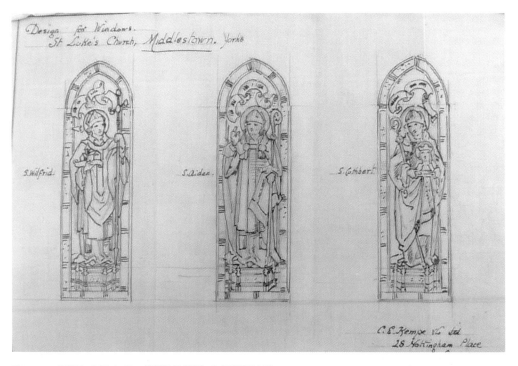

Diocese of *Wakefield Archive*, WYAS, Wakefield WD100

had simply dried up. What is more, by 1970, with the Vietnam War dominating headlines and the anti-war film *Oh, What a Lovely War!* playing in cinemas everywhere, stained glass memorials to the First World War were unlikely to be highly valued. Yet today the Middlestown glass, now restored and rearranged with the 1917 image of St. Oswald flanked by the later images of St Aidan and St Wilfrid, has a completeness and impact it lacked in its original context. St. Oswald would undoubtedly have been the central figure had he not already appeared in the 1917 window, and John Lisle must have regretted not being able to include him as the central figure; he would have been conscious that his trio of Northern saints had no obvious relevance to a war memorial. With his links to both Ripon and York, however, Wilfrid was an adequate regional substitute – though he was never an archbishop ('*Archepiscopus*' as Lisle labels him in an inscription in the window). It may even be that he was chosen at the request of the Kaye family, wanting a memorial to their son Wilfred. It is a happy irony, therefore, that only with Adam Goodyear's expert restoration and resetting of the glass has St. Luke's war memorial window finally achieved a focus and coherence it had lacked when first installed. Seen today, this Middlestown memorial glass demonstrates clearly the character and high quality of work produced by the Studio of C.E. Kempe & Co. during and soon after the Great War.

Restored War Memorial windows, St Luke's Church, Overton

INDEX